T0291343

BUSINESS PROCESS MODELING: SOFTWARE ENGINEERING, ANALYSIS AND APPLICATIONS

BUSINESS ISSUES, COMPETITION AND ENTREPRENEURSHIP

Additional books in this series can be found on Nova's website under the Series tab.

Additional E-books in this series can be found on Nova's website under the E-books tab.

BUSINESS PROCESS MODELING: SOFTWARE ENGINEERING, ANALYSIS AND APPLICATIONS

JASON A. BECKMANN
EDITOR

Nova Science Publishers, Inc.
New York

LIBRARY OF CONGRESS CATALOGING-IN-PUBLICATION DATA

Business process modeling : software engineering, analysis and applications / editors, Jason A. Beckmann.
    p. cm.
  Includes index.
  ISBN 978-1-61209-344-4 (hbk.)
  1. Management information systems. 2. Business--Data processing. 3.
Workflow--Management. I. Beckmann, Jason A.
  HD30.2.B8785 2010
  658.4'034--dc22
                              2010051515

Published by Nova Science Publishers, Inc. ✝ *New York*

CONTENTS

PREFACE

Business process modeling (BPM) is the activity of representing processes of an enterprise so that the current process may be analyzed and improved. BPM is typically performed by business analysts and managers who are seeking to improve process efficiency and quality. This book presents current research in the study of business process modeling, including BPM and automation with general and domain specific languages; conceptualizing, analyzing and communicating the business model and context-aware methods for process modeling.

Chapter 1 - Business Process Management (BPM) is an holistic approach for describing, analyzing, executing, managing and improving large enterprise business processes, which can be seen as collections of related tasks executed to accomplish well-defined goals.

This chapter focuses on the description and analysis of business processes. In particular, the chapter introduces a notation for the description of a business process in terms of both functional and non-functional properties. Such a description is then used to carry out the predictive analysis of the business process behaviour. The chapter specifically addresses the performance and reliability prediction of a business process by use of a joint measure known as performability.

In the BPM context, the Business Process Modeling Notation (BPMN) is the de-facto standard for the high-level description of business processes. Unfortunately BPMN does not support the characterization of the business process in terms of non-functional properties such as performance and reliability. To overcome such limitation, this chapter introduces PyBPMN (Performability-enabled BPMN), a lightweight BPMN extension for the specification of performability properties.

The proposed extension is based on an approach that exploits principles and standards introduced by MDA (Model Driven Architecture). In particular, the BPMN extension is carried out by first specifying the BPMN metamodel and then obtaining the PyBPMN metamodel by adding the metaclasses that define the specific performance and reliability characteristics.

The tasks that define a business process can be carried out either by human operators or by automated software services. This chapter specifically focuses on fully automated business processes that are defined and executed as orchestrations of software services. In this respect, PyBPMN can be used to describe the performance and reliability properties of both a business process and its constituent services.

This chapter also introduces a model-driven method that makes use of PyBPMN to predict, at design time, the performability of a business process, either to select the configuration of services that provide the best level of performability or to check if a given configuration satisfies the overall requirements of the business process. The proposed method can be fully automated, thus allowing business analysts to carry out the performability prediction with no extra effort and without being required to own specific skills of performability theory, as shown by use of an example case study.

Chapter 2 - A business model is a sustainable way of doing business. Here sustainability stresses the ambition to survive even harsh business landscapes and create profits in the long run. Whether profits are retained by the shareholders or distributed in some degree to a broader mass of stakeholders is not the focus here. Rather, it is the point of this paper to illustrate how one may go about conceptualizing, analyzing and communicating the business model of a company. A business model describes the coherence in the strategic choices which makes possible the handling of the processes and relations which create value on both the operational, tactical and strategic levels in the organization. The business model is the platform which connects resources, processes and the supply of a service, which results in the fact that the company is profitable in the long term. Conceptualizing the business model is therefore concerned with identifying this platform, while analyzing it is concerned with gaining an understanding of precisely which levers of control are apt to deliver the value proposition of the company. Finally, communicating the business model is concerned with identifying the most important performance measures, both absolute and relative measures, and relating them to the overall value creation story.

Chapter 3 - The role of business process models, as models in general, has been considerably changed from describing scenarios (contemplative models) towards actual coordinating activity execution (productive models) and from technical expert privilege to domain expert routine task.

Therefore, the challenge today is to reconcile two requirements: i) provide high level formalisms to domain experts, for the definition of models, and ii) execute these models, by mapping the abstract activities on various pieces of code and implementation artifacts. Automation of business processes, which is a pillar of nowadays frameworks evolvability, requires filling the gap between high level formalisms and execution. How this is performed is the topic of our chapter, which analyzes two approaches: the former based on large, general modeling languages, adopted as standards, and the latter based on small and composable domain specific languages. Examples of architectures driven by these process languages are presented, and solutions applied for the necessary transformations between different layers of abstraction are described.

Chapter 4 - This chapter proposes a view of business processes as designed artefacts that are ontologically no different than artefacts in domains such as mechanical and software engineering. This view distinguishes three concerns for designing processes: architecture, implementation and adaptation. The authors show that current process modelling approaches conflate these aspects, often leading to high complexity and inflexibility of the resulting process models. The authors use a generalisation of the "feature" concept in engineering design, represented using the function-behaviour-structure (FBS) ontology, as the basis of a new approach to concisely specifying business process architectures that allow for more process flexibility.

Chapter 5 - Recent studies have started to explore context-awareness as a driver in the design of adaptable business processes. The emerging challenge of identifying and considering contextual drivers in the environment of a business process are well understood, however, typical methods used in business process modeling do not yet consider this additional contextual information in their process designs. In this chapter, the authors describe our research towards innovative and advanced process modeling methods that include mechanisms to incorporate relevant contextual drivers and their impacts on business processes in process design models. The authors report on our ongoing work with an Australian insurance provider and describe the design science the authors employed to develop these innovative and useful artifacts as part of a context-aware method framework. The authors discuss the utility of these artifacts in an application in the claims handling process at the case organization.

Chapter 6 - Visual business process representation languages such as BPMN are a useful tool for specification of business processes. However, practical verification and execution of Business Process Models is a challenging task. One solution to this problem is integration of business processes with business rules, which provides a flexible runtime environment. This chapter concerns Business Process Models as a visual inference specification method for modularized rulebases. To provide the background for this approach, selected analysis and execution methods for Business Processes, such as BPEL and BPMN tools, are presented. Business Processes can be supported with Business Rules as executable logic. Rule-Based Systems have well-established methods for verification and optimization. This chapter presents selected rule-based solutions, such as Drools and XTT2 – a novel visual rule specification that provides formalized analysis – as well as their integration with BPMN as a visual method for inference specification. The proposed BPMN+XTT2 solution combines flexible business processmodeling provided by BPMN with verification and execution features of XTT2.

Chapter 7 - Business process modeling is an important stage in Business Process Management (BPM). There are many tools and methodologies to do such modeling. However, few of them can provide an optimal planning as well as the performance evaluation in a versatile environment. Since the globalized economics changes very fast, the process dynamics for each firm also changes day by day. Our approach can provide companies a helpful toolkit to manage such situation while keeping the ability to predict the performance of each business process. Due to IT advances in Enterprise Resource Planning Systems (ERPS), more and more companies adapted Service-Oriented Architecture (SOA) as the main infrastructure of their core business operations. So, process is the key identity of business activity to be monitored. However, how to capacitate (man or machine) as well as to evaluate the performance of such process, especially in a volatile environment, so that the business goal can be fulfilled is still unknow n to most of the mangers. This chapter proposes an integrated method to do both optimal capacity planning and performance evaluation for the companies facing people floating as well as system failures while keeping the capability to predict the performance of such process. So, the planning decision can be verified. A numerical example is illustrated for the proposed method.

In: Business Process Modeling   ISBN: 978-1-61209-344-4
Editor: Jason A. Beckmann   ©2011 Nova Science Publishers, Inc.

Chapter 1

PERFORMABILITY-ORIENTED DESCRIPTION AND ANALYSIS OF BUSINESS PROCESSES

*Paolo Bocciarelli and Andrea D'Ambrogio**
University of Rome "Tor Vergata", Rome, Italy

ABSTRACT

Business Process Management (BPM) is an holistic approach for describing, analyzing, executing, managing and improving large enterprise business processes, which can be seen as collections of related tasks executed to accomplish well-defined goals.

This chapter focuses on the description and analysis of business processes. In particular, the chapter introduces a notation for the description of a business process in terms of both functional and non-functional properties. Such a description is then used to carry out the predictive analysis of the business process behaviour. The chapter specifically addresses the performance and reliability prediction of a business process by use of a joint measure known as performability.

In the BPM context, the Business Process Modeling Notation (BPMN) is the de-facto standard for the high-level description of business processes. Unfortunately BPMN does not support the characterization of the business process in terms of non-functional properties such as performance and reliability. To overcome such limitation, this chapter

---

* {bocciarelli, dambro}@info.uniroma2.it

introduces PyBPMN (Performability-enabled BPMN), a lightweight BPMN extension for the specification of performability properties.

The proposed extension is based on an approach that exploits principles and standards introduced by MDA (Model Driven Architecture). In particular, the BPMN extension is carried out by first specifying the BPMN metamodel and then obtaining the PyBPMN metamodel by adding the metaclasses that define the specific performance and reliability characteristics.

The tasks that define a business process can be carried out either by human operators or by automated software services. This chapter specifically focuses on fully automated business processes that are defined and executed as orchestrations of software services. In this respect, PyBPMN can be used to describe the performance and reliability properties of both a business process and its constituent services.

This chapter also introduces a model-driven method that makes use of PyBPMN to predict, at design time, the performability of a business process, either to select the configuration of services that provide the best level of performability or to check if a given configuration satisfies the overall requirements of the business process. The proposed method can be fully automated, thus allowing business analysts to carry out the performability prediction with no extra effort and without being required to own specific skills of performability theory, as shown by use of an example case study.

1. INTRODUCTION

Business Process Management (BPM) is an holistic approach for describing, analyzing, executing, managing and improving large enterprise business processes, which can be seen as collections of related tasks executed to accomplish well-defined goals [4][31].

The term BPM is generally referred to the several activities that define the business process lifecycle [36]. This chapter specifically addresses the description of a business process and the use of such description for analyzing and predicting the process behaviour.

In the BPM context, the Business Process Modeling Notation (BPMN) is a standard, promoted by the Business Process Management Initiative (BPMI), for the high-level representation of business processes [21]. The main objective of the BPMI effort is the definition of a notation that has to be easily readable for the different people involved in the business process automation, namely, business analysts and designers who specify the business process and technical developers who implement the specified process.

Unfortunately, BPMN does not support the characterization of the business process in terms of non functional properties, such as performance and reliability. BPMN descriptions do not contain neither the specification of overall performance and reliability constraints (e.g., the response time associated to the entire business process execution, the process reliability, etc.), nor the specification of task properties (e.g., the mean time to failure of a single process task). This means that BPMN can be effectively used to define only the functional properties of a business process, without providing the ability to specify non-functional properties.

To overcome such limitation, this chapter introduces PyBPMN (Performability-enabled BPMN), a lightweight BPMN extension that addresses the specification of performance and reliability properties of a business process. The term performability is used to denote a joint property that combines performance and reliability [17][38].

The proposed extension is carried out according to principles and standards introduced in the model-driven engineering field and is specifically founded on the Meta Object Facility (MOF) [25], the standard for specifying technology neutral metamodels, and the XML Metadata Interchange (XMI) [24], the standard for serializing models and metamodels into XML documents and schemas, respectively. MOF and XMI are at the heart of the Model Driven Architecture (MDA), the OMG's incarnation of model-driven engineering principles [23].

The BPMN metamodel [22] is extended by adding the metaclasses needed to describe the performance and reliability properties, in order to obtain the novel PyBPMN metamodel. Both the BPMN metamodel and the PyBPMN metamodel are defined by use of MOF constructs. The PyBPMN XML Schema is then derived from the PyBPMN metamodel by use of XMI-based transformation rules.

The tasks that define a business process can be carried out either by human operators or by automated software services. This chapter addresses fully automated business processes that are defined and executed as orchestrations of software services. In this respect, PyBPMN can be used to describe the performability properties of both a business process and its constituent services.

The ability to specify the performability properties in the description of a business process is essential to predict its performance and reliability at design time. Such a prediction activity can effectively support business analysts to early identify performance and reliability problems, in order to compare different design alternatives and/or to select the best configuration of concrete services that implement the abstract tasks of a given abstract process.

The importance of a performability-based prediction activity is well known and widely recognized in the business process community, yet it is still far to be exploited in practice. This is due to several reasons, the most important one being its expensiveness in terms of costs and time. Traditionally, building a performability analysis model from a business process description requires a non negligible effort and significant skills in performance and reliability theory. Business analysts are usually not familiar with such theory and thus introducing a manual performability prediction activity is not convenient, from both cost and time-to-market points of view.

PyBPMN gives an essential contribution to produce business process specifications that can be mapped to performability analysis models by use of automated model transformations, thus overcoming the drawbacks of traditional model building activities.

In this respect, this chapter also introduces a model-driven method that exploits PyBPMN to predict, at design time, the performability of a business process, either to select the configuration of services that provide the best level of performability or to check if a given configuration satisfies the overall performability requirements of the business process.

The proposed method takes as input the BPMN specification of a business process and makes use of the extended PyBPMN specification to carry out the business process analysis that yields the performability prediction. The method is based on a set of model transformations first to obtain a model that gives the UML (Unified Modeling Language) representation of the business process and then to derive the performance and reliability models whose evaluation yields the performability prediction.

The translation of a BPMN-based description into a UML-based representation is essential to benefit from previous contributions [7][8][10] that provide model-driven methods for automatically building performance and reliability models, as detailed in Sections 0 and 0, respectively. The evaluation of such models yields the performance and reliability predictions that contribute to obtain the performability prediction of a business process.

In addition, the use of UML allows to take advantage of specific UML extensions, called profiles, that provide a standard approach for annotating UML models with domain-specific information. Specifically, the proposed method makes use of both the MARTE profile [27], for annotating performance and reliability information, and the SoaML profile [28], for annotating information that characterize the SOA-based implementation of a business process.

All such transformations are specified by use of the QVT (Query/View/Transformation) language [29], which is provided by the OMG as the standard language for specifying model transformations that can be executed by a given QVT engine [13].

In order to define an integrated BMPN- and SOA-based approach for specifying, analyzing and implementing business processes, the model-driven method also includes an additional model transformation that is executed to generate the BPEL (Business Process Execution Language) code from the PyBPMN description, according to the algorithm proposed in [21][19].

The main advantage of the proposed model-driven method is that business analysts are allowed to automate the performability analysis of a given business process with no extra effort and without being required to own specific skills of performability theory, as shown by use of an example case study.

The rest of the chapter is organized as follows: Section 2 gives background concepts about BPM, to better frame the context of this chapter contribution. Section 4 describes PyBPMN, i.e., the proposed BPMN extension. Section 5 presents the method that exploits PyBPMN to enable the model-driven performability prediction of a business process, and, finally Section 6 gives an example application.

2. BPM BACKGOUND CONCEPTS

This section outlines a set of reference standards and technologies used in the BPM context, to better frame this chapter scope and contribution.

In particular, the next subsections illustrate the role of SOA-based technologies in the BPM context, the standard BPMN for the specification of business processes and the standard BPEL for the execution of business processes onto SOA-based execution platforms, respectively.

2.1 BPM and Service Oriented Architectures (SOAs)

In order to achieve the highest degree of agility and efficiency, BPM is supported by IT-based standards and technologies, such as Service Oriented Architectures (SOAs) [34] and Web Services [1]. The automated execution of tasks within a business process, from the implementation perspective, is often founded on the Web Services technology. Web services represent just a set of technologies needed to invoke remote services, while SOA standards "enables the independent construction of services which can be combined to realize meaningful, higher level business process within the context of the enterprise", as stated in [37]. In other words a business process can be executed over an application platform defined in terms of a SOA by use of the Web Service implementation technology, as depicted in Figure 1, which separates the business process specification (upper part) from the implementation and execution onto the underlying application platform (bottom part).

The business process consists of a set of abstract tasks that are mapped (see dashed lines in Figure 1) to a set of services, denoted as *business services*, which provide the actual task operation. In a SOA context such business services are implemented as web services executed on top of a platform that provides the set of required operational resources.

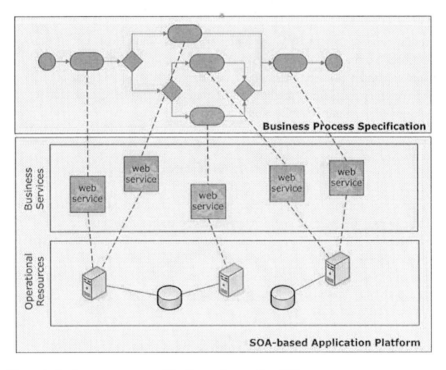

Figure 1. Business process specification and execution [37].

In the scenario depicted in Figure 1, a business process is executed as a SOA-based composition of web services. The set of services is composed according to the orchestration pattern, that identifies a central authority (or coordinator) in charge of managing the web services invocation and execution [35].

In the rest of the chapter, the term component (or atomic) web service denotes the web service that implements a single abstract task of the business process, while the term composite web service denotes the orchestration of a set of component web services. Thus the implementation of a business process can be seen as the implementation of a composite web service.

In this perspective, it is essential to point out how a business process can be described at different levels of abstraction, from analysis and design to implementation. To this purpose, the following sections describe the BPMN and the BPEL standards, respectively.

2.2 Business Process Management Notation (BPMN)

As already mentioned in Section 1, the Business Process Modeling Notation (BPMN) is a standard promoted by the Business Process Management Initiative (BPMI) for the high-level representation of business processes. One of the main objectives of BPMI is the definition of a graphical notation that results effective and easily understandable by business process analysts and designers. BPMN is typically used at the early stages of the process lifecycle, i.e., to define analysis and design models of the business process, and then used to drive the implementation of the business process.

The business process description is carried out by building business process diagrams (BPDs), which are composed of flow objects, i.e., the core elements provided by BPMN. Flow objects can be events, activities and gateways. An activity represents a step (i.e., a generic piece of work) in the business process and can be either atomic (task) or compound (sub-process). An event represents the start or the end of a process. A gateway specifies the divergence and convergence of execution flows, in order to model the several kinds of branching in execution flows (i.e., decisions, fork, join, merge, etc.). BPDs also include four types of connecting objects: sequence flows, depicted as solid arrows and used to connect together the flow objects to create the structure of the business process; message flow, depicted as dashed arrows, and used to show the flow of messages between two different participants (i.e., business entities responsible of task execution) and finally associations, represented as dotted arrows, and used to link information to the flow objects. For a detailed description of BPMN the reader is referred to the official specification [21].

One of the major advantages resulting from the adoption of BPMN for the specification of high level business processes is that BPMN can be translated into BPEL, reducing the gap that exists between the business specialists domain and the IT specialists domains [30][31][32][33]. Business specialists are responsible for the business process specification phase, that focuses on the abstract representation of the business process, while the later phases such as the design, implementation and execution of the business process are typically IT-related activities.

2.3 Business Process Execution Language (BPEL)

As aforementioned, BPMN gives a notation to represent a business process from an abstract point of view. The implementation of a business process described by BPMN can be carried out by use of SOA-based technologies through the composition of a set of web services.

The Business Process Execution Language for Web Services (BPEL) is the de-facto standard for the SOA-based execution of business processes [33][31]. BPEL has been jointly created by IBM, BEA and Microsoft in August 2002 and then submitted to OASIS (Organization for the Advancement of Structured Information Standards) to obtain open standardization [18].

BPEL represents a convergence of the ideas in XLANG (a block structured process language) [39] and WSFL (a graph-based process language) specifications [16], which have been superseded by the BPEL specification. A BPEL process is an XML document typically generated by use of visual tools. The XML document describes the BPEL process in terms of both process logic and invocation of external services. The main element of a BPEL process is called activity and represents a step involved in the business process. A BPEL process is executed by an orchestration engine that takes as input the XML document and coordinates the process activities. The BPEL process can in turn be exposed as an actual service that can be invoked through a standard web service interface.

A BPEL document can be automatically obtained from a BPMN-based business process specification. The automatic translation of BPMN into BPEL is part of the performability prediction method proposed in this chapter, as described in Section 0.

3. PERFORMABILITY-ENABLED BPMN (PYBPMN)

This section introduces the Performability-enabled BPMN (PyBPMN), a BPMN extension for the performability-oriented annotations of BPDs.

The extension process is described in Section 0, while Section 0 and Section 0 describe the BPMN metamodel and the PyBPMN metamodel, respectively.

3.1 Metamodel Extension Process

As said in Section 1, the proposed extension has been carried out as a metamodel transformation, according to principles and standards recommended by MDA.

The set of guidelines provided by MDA strongly relies on metamodeling techniques for structuring specifications expressed as models and transformations between such models [23]. In this respect, MOF is the key standard that provides an abstract language and a framework for specifying, constructing, and managing technology neutral metamodels, or models used to describe other models [25]. In MDA terms, a model (e.g., an UML model [26]) is an instance of a MOF metamodel (e.g., the UML metamodel [26]), which in turn is an instance of the MOF meta-metamodel specified in [24] (and briefly called MOF Model).

A side standard of MOF is the OMG's XMI specification, which provides a set of rules to serialize models and MOF metamodels into XML documents and XML Schemas, respectively, and to derive a MOF metamodel from an XML Schema [24].

The extension process, illustrated in Figure 2, leverages on MOF and XMI and is based on a metamodel extension that, according to the MOF metamodeling architecture, is defined at the metamodel layer.

As a consequence, both the BPMN and the PyBPMN metamodels are represented in terms of MOF primitives.

The first step of the process is the BPMN metamodel extension, that takes as input the MOF metamodel of BPMN and yields as output the MOF metamodel of PyBPMN.

A MOF metamodel is represented in terms of MOF primitives such as classes, attributes and associations. The representation of the BPMN syntax in terms of its MOF metamodel facilitates its comprehension and makes its extension easier.

The PyBPMN metamodel is easily obtained by adding metaclasses that extend the original ones, without applying any modifications to the BPMN metamodel. This has also the advantage of maintaining a complete backward compatibility with BPMN, so that a BPMN model conforms to both the BPMN and PyBPMN metamodels.

The second step of the extension process is the serialization of the PyBPMN metamodel by use of the XMI Schema Production Rules, in order to obtain the PyBPMN schema. The XMI Document Production Rules are instead used to derive the PyBPMN document, which is basically a XML document, from the corresponding PyBPMN model. According to what stated before for a BPMN model, a BPMN XML document is valid with respect to both the BPMN and the PyBPMN XML Schemas.

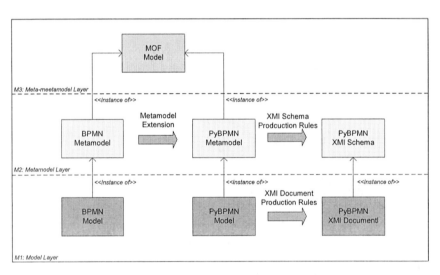

Figure 2. PyBPMN extension process.

It is worth noting that the currently available BPMN specification, version 1.2 [19], does not include a MOF compliant BPMN metamodel definition. The MOF compliance is a requirement of the RFP for BPMN version 2 [20]. At the moment of writing this chapter, OMG has released the BPMN 2.0 Beta 1 specification [21] that, according to the aforementioned RFP, includes a detailed description of the MOF BPMN metamodel. The PyBPMN metamodel extension proposed in this chapter is based on this last specification.

3.2 BPMN Metamodel

Figure 3 illustrates the portion of the BPMN metamodel that describes the relationship among the most relevant metamodel elements, specifically those involved in the extension process. A complete description of the BPMN metamodel is out of the scope of this chapter. For a complete description the reader is sent to the BPMN specification [21].

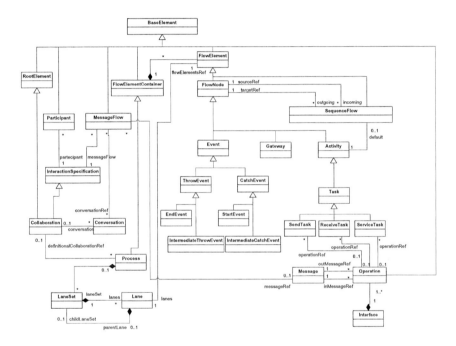

Figure 3. MOF metamodel of BPMN.

As aforementioned, a BPMN process is graphically represented by use of a BPD that defines the execution semantics as a graph in which nodes are flow objects (i.e., events, activities and gateways) and arcs are connecting objects (specifically sequence flows and message flows).

The most relevant elements in the BPMN metamodel are the metaclasses Process, MessageFlow, FlowNode and SequenceFlow.

The Process metaclass, that inherits from FlowElementContainer metaclass, models the sequence of flow elements (e.g., activities) in a process. Note that while the Process metaclass is specifically used to represent the set of flow elements, the interaction between processes is represented by use of Collaboration metaclass.

The MessageFlow metaclass is used to represent the interaction that takes place as exchange of messages between two participants within a collaboration.

FlowNode is the superclass of the metaclasses Event, Activity and Gateway. The relationship among two flow objects connected by a sequence flow is represented by the associations between SequenceFlow and FlowNode metaclasses.

Activity metaclass, which is refined by a Task metaclass, represents a step in the business process. Figure 3 only gives the most relevant metaclasses which specialize the Task metaclass. The ServiceTask metaclass represents a Task that is executed automatically (i.e., by use of a Web service or an automated application). The SendTask and ReceiveTask metaclasses represent tasks involved in an exchange of messages among different participants.

3.3 PyBPMN Metamodel

In order to enrich the BPMN metamodel with the information required to carry out the performability analysis, the UML Profile for Modeling and Analysis of Real-Time Embedded systems (MARTE) [27] has been taken under consideration. The MARTE profile is limited to the description of performance attributes without providing any support for reliability analysis. To this purpose, the proposed BPMN extension is also inspired by additional contributions that add the description of reliability properties to the MARTE profile [5] [6].

In this chapter case, the concepts introduced in [5][6][27] have been adapted and used to derive the metaclasses of the PyBPMN metamodel[1]. The extension can ideally be divided into three main directions:

> ➢ workload definition: to specify the workload for both the collaboration diagram (that represents the business process

---

[1] It is worth to note that the main goal is not to provide an exhaustive catalog for the description of performance and reliability properties of web services, but to illustrate a method in which the characteristics defined by an UML Profile can be used to enrich the WSDL description in order to be applied to a given domain. Additional characteristics can be defined or existing ones be modified or removed to fit specific needs. The fact that the extension process can be fully automate makes its customization easy to carry out.

implemented as a composite web services), and one of processes associated to the collaboration (corresponding to the providers of the component services). The workload is specified by use of the GaWorkloadEvent and the ArrivalPattern metaclasses;

➢ performance properties definition: to model the performance properties associated to the collaboration, the related processes and/or the single task, in terms of response time, throughput and CPU demand. Performance properties are specified by use of the PaQualification metaclass;

➢ reliability properties definition: to represent the reliability properties at process and/or at task level. Reliability properties are specified by the use of the DaQualification metaclasses (i.e., DaFault, DaFailure and DaError).

The portions of the PyBPMN metamodel shown in Figure 4 and Figure 5 describe the extensions addressing the workload definition and the performability (performance and reliability) properties definition, respectively. Metaclasses and associations that have been added to extend the BPMN metamodel are highlighted by use of a gray background.

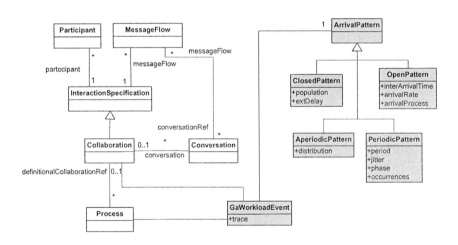

Figure 4. PyBPMN extension for workload characterization.

PyBPMN introduces the following additional metaclasses into the BPMN metamodel:

- GaWorkloadEvent: to model the stream of requests representing the workload. It is characterized by the optional trace attribute that specifies the name of the file storing the trace (i.e., the request event stream that specifies the workload).
- Pattern: to specify the arrival pattern (periodic, aperiodic, closed, open) and the related characteristics.
- DaError: to represent a property related to the errors that may affect the system implementing the business process. It is specified by the following attributes:

  o   latency: time elapsed between the error occurrence and the subsequent detection;
  o   probability: probability of an error occurrence.

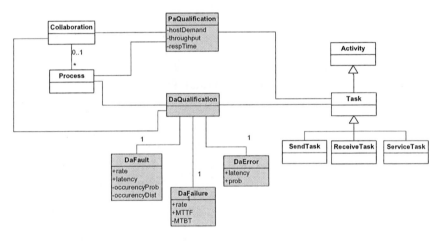

Figure 5. PyBPMN extension for performance and reliability characterization.

- DaFault: to representsa requirement related to the faults that may affect the system. It is specified by the following attributes:

  o   rate: the fault occurrence rate. The type of this attribute is the complex data type DaFrequency, described below;
  o   occurency Prob: probability of a fault occurrence;
  o   occurency Dist: probability distribution of fault occurrences.

- DaFailure: to represent a requirement (or a constraint) related to the failures that may affect the system. It is specified by the following attributes:

  o rate: failure occurrency rate. The type of this attribute is the complex data type DaFrequency, described below.
  o MTTF: mean time to failure. The attribute type is NFP_Duration, specified below.
  o MTBF: mean time between failures. The attribute type is NFP_Duration, specified below.

- PaQualification: to represent a requirement related to the performance of a single task or of the system that implements the entire business process. This metaclass does not have a direct corresponding element in MARTE, but it is defined by merging the concepts modelled by PaStep, GaStep and GaScenario elements. It is specified by the following attributes:

  o executionDemand: execution demand in terms of units of time, required for the execution of a single task or an entire process, if all the related steps are executed on the same host. The type of this attribute is the complex data type NFP_Duration, described below;
  o troughput: throughput related to the associated task/process. The type of this attribute is the complex data type NFP_Frequency, described below;
  o resp Time: response time for the related task/process. The type of this attribute is the complex data type NFP_Duration, described below.

The set of metaclasses introduced by PyBPMN makes use of the following datatypes:

- DaFrequency: to represent rate attributes. It is specified by the following attributes:

  o unit: unit of measure of the attribute. It is an enumerated data type that can assume the values specified in [6], i.e. fail/s, fail/month, fault/day, etc.;

- o   precision: degree of precision in the performance of a measurement operation.

- NFP_Duration: represents time-related attributes such as MTTF or MTBF. It is specified by the following attributes:

    - o   unit: unit of measure of the attribute. It is an enumerated data type that can assume the following values: s, tick, ms, us, min, hrs, days;
    - o   precision: degree of precision in the performance of a measurement operation;
    - o   value: value of the attribute.

- NFP_Frequency: this it is specified by the following attributes:

    - o   unit: the unit of measure of the attribute. It is an enumerated data type that can assume the following values: Hz, KHz, MHz, GHz;
    - o   precision: degree of precision in the performance of a measurement operation;
    - o   value: value of the attribute.

The above illustrated set of datatypes extends the NFP_CommonType (see [5][27]), which represents the basic structure of a complex data type, specified by the following attributes:

- expr: an expression specified in MARTE Value Specification Language (VSL) [27];
- source: specifies the origin of the attribute. It is an enumerated data type that can assume the following values: estimated, calculated, required or measured;
- statQ: qualifies the type of statistical value. It is an enumerated data type that can assume the following values: maximum, minimum, mean, percentile, distribution or other;
- dir: defines the type of order relation used to compare value. It is an enumerated data type that can assume the following values: increasing or decreasing.

As outlined in Section 0, PyBPMN is used to describe an abstract business process that is taken as input by the performability prediction method illustrated in the next section. Thanks to PyBPMN, the abstract model can be enriched with data that specify properties and the constraints related to performance and reliability characteristics.

Figure 6 gives an example use of PyBPMN to produce a PyBPMN model in which the performability properties of a business process are annotated, while Figure 7 gives the corresponding XML document, obtained from the PyBPMN model by use of XMI document production rules (see Figure 2).

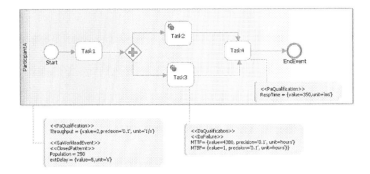

Figure 6. Example PyBPMN model.

```
<bpmn2:definitions xmi:version="2.0" xmlns:xmi=http://www.omg.org/XMI ...>

    ...

    <reusableElement xsi:type="bpmn2:collaboration" id="... " name="Example">

        <gaworkloadevent>

            <closedpattern popupation="25", extDelay= " (value=5, unit='ms') "/>

        </gaworkload>

        <paqualification respTime="(value=350, unit='ms')"/ >

        ...

    </reusableElement >

    <reusableElement xsi:type="bpmn2:process" id="..." name="Process1">

        <flowElement xsi:type="bpmn2:startEvent" id="..." name="Start" />

        <flowElement xsi:type="bpmn2:task" id="..." name="Task1" />

        <flowElement xsi:type="bpmn2:sequenceFlow" id="..." sourceRef="... " targetRef="..." />

        <flowElement xsi:type="bpmn2:parallelGateway" id="..." name="" />
```

Figure 7. Example PyBPMN model serialized into XML (portion).

4. PᴜBPMN-Bᴀsᴇᴅ Pᴇʀꜰᴏʀᴍᴀʙɪʟɪᴛʏ Pʀᴇᴅɪᴄᴛɪᴏɴ ᴏꜰ Bᴜsɪɴᴇss Pʀᴏᴄᴇssᴇs

This section describes the proposed approach for the performability prediction of business processes. The approach first specifies the business process in terms of a PyBPMN model, that defines the non functional performability properties as well as the (abstract) steps composing the business process, and then binds each abstract task to a (concrete) web service that provides its implementation. The business process is thus implemented as an orchestration of web services.

At design time several alternatives of the business process may be available, corresponding to different bindings of abstract tasks to available concrete services. Business analysts and designers may be thus interested to compare the different alternatives in order to identify the configuration that provides the best overall performability and/or to answer what-if questions. At the same time the ability to describe the performability properties of a business process allows to better qualify the offer and gain a significant advantage in the global marketplace.

Figure 8 illustrates the proposed method, which exploits PyBPMN and enables business analysts and designers to carry out an effective performability prediction at design   time, starting from the abstract business process specification.

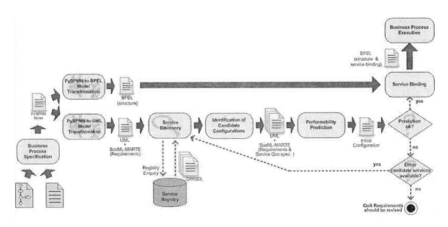

Figure 8. Method for performability prediction at design time.

The method is inspired by the one illustrated in [7] and is integrated into a complete model-driven service composition process, which consists of activities that take as input and/or produce as output XML documents representing various types of documents, e.g., PyBPMN models, UML models, performance models and BPEL documents.

The business process is initially specified in terms of its abstract model, described by means of PyBPMN. Beyond the specification of functional properties, PyBPMN allows the definition of non-functional (i.e., performability-related in the chapter case) properties and constraints.

The PyBPMN model is initially translated into both a BPEL document and an UML document by use of two different model transformations, namely, the PyBPMN-to-BPEL transformation and the PyBPMN-to-UML transformation.

The PyBPMN-to-BPEL transformation is carried out according to the algorithm proposed in [21] and is implemented as described in [31]. It should be noted that at this step the binding operation has not yet been performed and thus there are no information about the concrete services that will implement the business process tasks. For such a reason the transformation only produces the structure of the BPEL document. The information needed to invoke the concrete services will be added to the BPEL just after the execution of the binding operation, as described afterward.

The PyBPMN-to-UML transformation is specified in QVT [29] and executed onto a QVT engine [13]. The transformation takes as input the PyBPMN model and yields as output an implementation-oriented UML model that gives a standard description of the SOA-based orchestration implementing the business process. The UML model is annotated according to both the SoaML profile, to define the SOA-based architecture specification, and the MARTE profile, to specify the performability properties. The UML model consists of the following set of packages, according to the modeling conventions for the application of the SoaML profile [2]:

> ➢ Service Interface Package: to specify the abstract interfaces that the concrete services must implement in order to be involved in the business process orchestration.
> ➢ Participant Package: to define the relationship among the Participants (i.e., a person, a system or an organization that provides or consumes a service, in SoaML terms) that implement the abstract interfaces defined above.
> ➢ Service Contract Package: to define the Service Contracts (i.e., the specification of agreements between interacting parties, in SoaML terms).

➢ Service Architecture Package: to specify the Service Architecture (i.e., the network of participants providing and consuming services to achieve a goal, associated with the specification of the business process defining the related orchestration, in SoaML terms), by means of an UML collaboration diagram enriched with a nested UML activity diagram that describes the flow of activities carried out to enact the business process.

A service discovery is then carried out, in order to retrieve a set of concrete services that match the abstract services interfaces. Specifically, the service discovery retrieves a set of Q-WSDL descriptions of the concrete services[2]. In general, the service discovery step gives as output more than a single concrete service for each abstract service. Thus, the next step in Figure 8 deals with the identification of candidate configurations, in other words the set of different configurations that represent the possible bindings obtained from the set of available concrete services. As an example, the right side of Figure 9 shows the two candidate configurations that can be identified when binding the abstract task 3 of the business process on the left side to the concrete services C and E, respectively.

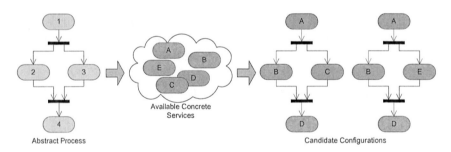

Figure 9. Identification of candidate configurations after service discovery.

From the set of candidate configurations it is then necessary to select the initial configuration. The proposed method carries out such selection by use of a performability prediction activity, which yields as output the quantitative indices for selecting the initial configuration that provides the best level of performability among the set of identified candidate configurations.

---

2 Q-WSDL is a lightweight WSDL extension used to describe the performance and reliability properties of the component web services whose orchestration yields the composite web service implementing a business process. The reader is sent to [11] for a detailed description of Q-WSDL.

The performability prediction activity consists of two prediction activities that separately deal with performance and reliability properties, respectively, and a subsequent aggregate prediction that yields the performability indices of interest, as illustrated in Figure 10 and detailed in Sections 0 through 0. The prediction activity takes as input the set of UML models corresponding to the set of candidate configurations. Such UML models specify the performability properties of both the business process and the concrete services of the corresponding candidate binding.

The so obtained performability prediction can be used to check whether the predicted level meets the desired or required level of performability.

In such a case, a service binding activity is carried out to produce the BPEL document that specifies both the already available abstract structure and the binding data that identify the concrete services implementing the abstract tasks. The complete BPEL document is finally given as input to the BPEL orchestration engine that is in charge of executing the business process (e.g., Apache Orchestration Director Engine [3]).

In case the predicted level of performability is not satisfactory, a new service discovery activity can be carried out to check if additional services are available for identifying and evaluating alternative candidate configurations.

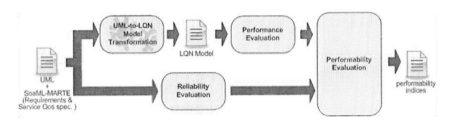

Figure 10. Details of the performability prediction in Figure 8.

4.1 Performance Prediction

The performance prediction activity takes as input the UML models of the different candidate configurations and yields as output the performance prediction for each candidate configuration.

The performance prediction is carried out by first translating the annotated UML model into a performance model and then by evaluating the performance model in order to obtain the performance indices of the business process, such as response time, throughput or resource utilization. The automated building of performance models from UML models has been widely investigated as a valid tool for predicting the performance of software systems, and several contributions are available in literature (see, e.g., [10][12][14][42]).

In this chapter case, the obtained performance model is of LQN (Layered Queueing Network) type [41]. LQN models give a powerful formalism to define models that takes into account the scalability issues related to the resource contention of software/hardware resources.

The performance prediction activity thus consists of a UML-to-LQN model transformation and a subsequent LQN model evaluation.

The UML-to-LQN model transformation, is specified by use of a declarative approach that describes how UML patterns are transformed into the corresponding LQN patterns, as described in full details in [10].

The so-obtained LQN model is given as input to a LQN solver [15], which carries out the model evaluation step and yields as output the predictions about the performance of the business process.

According to the method illustrated in Figure 8, the performance prediction activity has to be carried out for each candidate configuration that specifies a possible binding of concrete services. The UML models corresponding to the different candidate configurations are identical from a structural point of view and only differ for the performance properties specified by MARTE-based model annotations. This is reflected in LQN models as well, which only differ in terms of parameterization.

As a result, after the inital model transformation that yields the LQN model corresponding to the UML model of the initial candidate configuration, the additional LQN models corresponding to the UML models of remaining candidate configurations are simply obtained by means of a different parameterization, without any modifications to the structure of the initial LQN model. This achieves significant savings in terms of efficiency of the performance prediction activity.

4.2 Reliability Prediction

The reliability prediction activity takes as input the UML models of the different candidate configurations and yields as output the reliability prediction for each candidate configuration.

In particular, the UML activity diagram (AD) that represents the business process behavior is taken as input. An activity diagram is used to describe the business process as a graph consisting of a start node that initiates the process, a series of intermediate nodes that represent both process activities and decision nodes, a final node that terminates the process and a set of edges that detail the many decision paths that exist in the sequence of activities.

The reliability prediction is carried out by use of an algorithm that iteratively applies a set of reduction rules until only a single atomic AD node remains. The algorithm, inspired by [9], proceeds by iteratively applying the reduction rules shown in Table 1.

Table 1. Reduction rules for the reliability prediction.

Pattern	Reduction Rule	Notes
Sequence	$R_{sequence}(t) = \prod_{i=1}^{Ns} R_i(t)$	Ri(t) denotes the realibility associated to the i-th node in the sequence; Ns is the number of nodes in the sequence.
Loop	$R_{loop}(t) = R_a(t)^k$	Ri(t) denotes the realibility associated to the node a; k is the number of iteration in the loop.
Parallel flow	$R_{flow}(t) = \prod_{i=1}^{nf} R_i(t)$	R$_i$(t) denotes the realibility associated to the i-th node in the flow; Nf is the number of braches.
Switch	$R_{switch}(t) = \sum_{i=1}^{Nsw} p_i * R_i(t)$	Ri(t) denotes the realibility associated to the i-th node in the flow; pi is the probability of execution associated to the i-th branches; Nsw is the number of braches.

According to a widely accepted assumption [40], the failures of the different services, and of their relevant operations, are independent. By assuming an exponential distribution probability for the failures in the business process, the reliability associated to each AD node a, can be computed as:

$$R_a(t) = e^{-\frac{1}{MTTF_a}t}$$

(1)

where $R_a(t)$ and $MTTF_a$ are the reliability and the mean time to failure associated to the node a of the AD, respectively. A detailed description of the reliability prediction algorithm can be found in [8].

The structure of the annotated AD changes at each iteration and after a number of iterations it is reduced to a single node. When this state is reached, the reliability associated to the remaining node specifies the reliability of the composite web service that implements the service process described by the AD under analysis.

4.3 Performability Prediction

Let us consider n different candidate configurations BP_i (i=1..n) of a business process BP, resulting from a service discovery activity that retrieves more than one concrete service to be bound to each abstract service of the abstract model. Each configuration may be analyzed by use of the methods illustrated in the previous sections in order to obtain the prediction that leads to an optimal choice of the initial configuration in terms of either performance or reliability.

At this time, it is quite usual to find conflicting predictions, in other words the optimal configuration estimated in terms of performance is not the optimal one in terms of reliability and vice versa. This claims for a joint analysis of performance and reliability so that the comparison of different design alternatives, such as which one to adopt as initial configuration, may be then based on predictions of the combined attribute known as performability.

The performability prediction is carried out by use of the following algorithm [7]:

1. generate the state transition diagram STD associated with the Markov chain that represents the possible configurations which the business process implementation may undergo before experimenting a failure (this implies that when a service fails and a working service providing the same functionality is available, the business process implementation switch to a new configuration that includes the working service);
2. select a candidate configuration as the initial configuration;
3. use the reliability prediction method illustrated in Section 0 to obtain the transition probabilities of the STD;

4. calculate the absorbing probabilities $P(BP_i)$ of being in a given working configuration $(i=1..n)$ starting from the initial configuration;
5. use the performance prediction method illustrated in Section 0 to obtain the performance associated to each configuration, e.g., in terms of its throughput $T(BP_i)$, and assign it as a reward to the configuration;
6. obtain the performability prediction in terms of the *expected reward rate* of BP as:

$$RW(BP) = \sum_{i=1}^{n} P(BP_i)T(BP_i) \qquad (2)$$

where:

> - RW(BP) is the expected reward rate of the business process, i.e., an overall attribute that combines both performance and reliability;
> - $P(BP_i)$ is the probability of the system to be in the *i-th* working configuration starting from the initial configuration, as computed by means of STD;
> - $T(BP_i)$ is the throughput of the *i-th* candidate configuration.

The comparison among the so obtained reward rates for each candidate initial configuration allows to carry out a choice that takes into account both the performance and the reliability of the composite service.

The next section illustrates an example application of the proposed method, in order to give an actual concretization of what described in Section 0.

5. EXAMPLE APPLICATION

This section shows how the proposed model-driven method exploits PyBPMN to predict, at design time, the performability of an example business process. It is assumed that the example business process deals with travel planning, in analogy to [7].

In the example business process, a *travel plan* is built through the following main steps:

1. flight information and hotel accommodation are retrieved;
2. car renting information is retrieved;
3. transportation from airport to the hotel (and vice versa) is planned; depending on the user preferences, the plan may include either a timetable of airport shuttles or an estimated cab fare.

As regards step 3, it is assumed that an average 70% customers prefer a cab rather than an airport shuttle. The preliminary abstract business process is shown in Figure 11.

The following web services are required to implement the travel plan business process:

*   a service providing information about flight availability and reservation, denoted as flights manager (FM) service;
*   a service providing information about hotel reservation and airport services (e.g., timetables of airport shuttles), denoted as accommodation manager (AM) service;
*   a service providing information about car renting and cab fare estimates, denoted as transportation manager (TM) service.

By use of PyBPMN the business process diagram is enriched with the performability properties summarized in Table 3. Such properties give the constraints that must be met by the business process implementation. For example, the execution of the Travel Plan business process must be completed in no more than 2.5 seconds. The resulting PyBPMN diagram is shown in Figure 12.

Table 2. Performability properties.

	Addressed Process/Task	Constraint
Performance	Travel Plan process	execution time ≤ 2500ms
	Flight Reservation task	execution time ≤ 300ms
Reliability	Travel Plan process	MTTF ≥ 7000 hours
	Travel Plan process	MTTR ≤ 8 hours
	Hotel Reservation task	MTTF ≥ 6500 hours

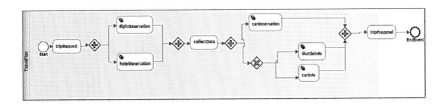

Figure 11. BPMN diagram (abstract business process).

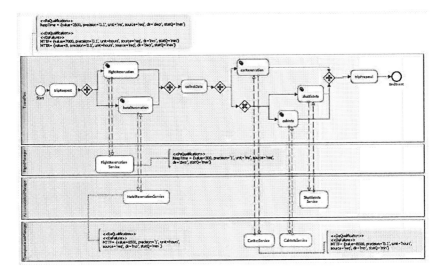

Figure 12. PyBPMN diagram (abstract BP with performability annotations).

The method illustrated in Figure 8 takes as input the PyBPMN description and yields as output the performability prediction.

At the first step, the PyBPMN-to-UML model transformation obtains the UML model annotated with SoaML and MARTE profiles. The so obtained UML model consists of:

- a class diagram showing the abstract interfaces that the concrete services must implement, as shown in Figure 13;
- a collaboration diagram that shows the involved Participants and their interactions specified by means of Service Contract Use, as shown in Figure 14;
- an activity diagram that specifies the behaviour of the business process, annotated by use of the MARTE profile, as shown in Figure 15. The example annotations refer to a possible binding of

the abstract task to concrete services that provide the performance and reliability values shown in Figure 15.

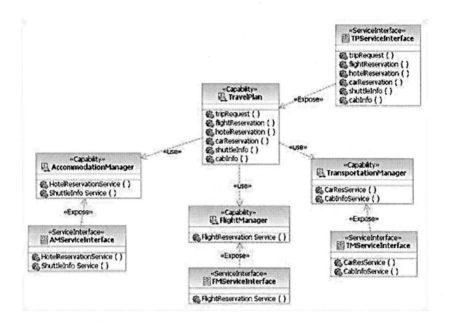

Figure 13. Capabilities and Service Interfaces.

At the second step, a service discovery is carried out to find a set of concrete services that match both the abstract service interfaces and the performance and reliability constraints specified in the PyBPMN (as shown in Table 2 and Figure 12).

For the sake of simplicity, it is supposed that a single concrete service is found for AM and FM services, while two different concrete services are available for binding the TM service. Table 3 summarizes the performance and reliability data extracted from the Q-WSDL documents of the two alternative services, namely TM_A and TM_B.

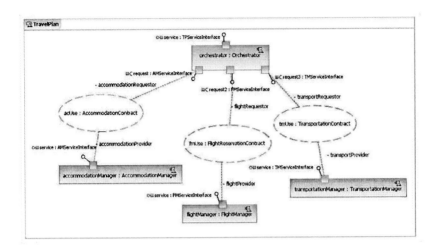

Figure 14. Collaboration Diagram defining the SOA.

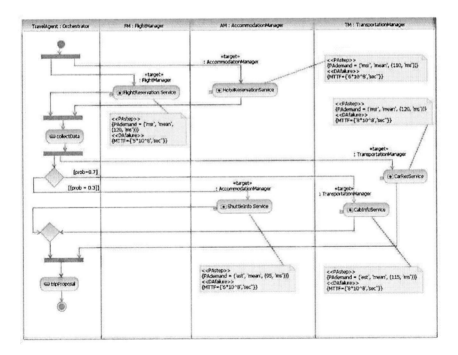

Figure 15. Activity Diagram.

Table 3. Data obtained from Q-WSDL documents.

Parameter		TM_A	TM_B
Performance	Car Reservation time demand	120 ms	90 ms
	CabInfo time demand	115 ms	84 ms
	Network bit rate	10 Mb	100 Mb
Reliability	MTTF	$10*10^8$ hours	$7.2*10^7$ hours
	R(1year)	0.961	0.645

As described in Section 0, the annotated AD is then used to conduct the performability analysis, by first predicting the performance and reliability properties and then combining the two predictions into an overall performability prediction.

Figure 16 summarizes the results of the performance prediction, as obtained by the prediction method described in Section 0. The figures show the service time of the two different composite services that implement the business service by including TM_A and TM_B, respectively, for different values of the number of service consumers. It should be noted that both configurations satisfy the global constraint related to the performance shown in Table 2 (specifically, the execution time for the Travel Plan process must be shorter than 2500 msec), but for a different maximum number of service consumers (25 and 30 users, respectively). This result leads to argue that the alternative denoted as TM_B is to be preferred if the prediction is limited to the performance characteristics of the composite service.

The results of the reliability prediction are shown in Table 4, that gives the estimated reliability for the composite services with TM_A and TM_B. The reliability values have been obtained by use of the prediction method described in Section 0, while the corresponding MTTF values have been derived by use of equation (1).

It is easy to see that even if the prediction takes into account only the reliability characteristics of the business process, the results summarized in Table 4 show that both the configurations including TM_A and TM_B satisfy the global constraints shown in Table 2 but, in contrast with the performance prediction results, the alternative denoted as TM_A is the one to be preferred.

Table 4. Reliability prediction results.

BP implementation	Reliability	MTTF
Candidate Configuration with TM_A	0.746	$1,8*10^8$ hours
Candidate Configuration with TM_B	0.385	$3,3*10^7$ hours

This simple case motivates the need of conducting a joint analysis of performance and reliability attributes in order to determine the initial configuration to be chosen from both a performance and a reliability point of view. This joint evaluation is obtained by use of the method described in Section 0 and is quantified in terms of the expected reward rate for the business processes with TM_A and TM_B. The obtained results are shown in Figure 17.

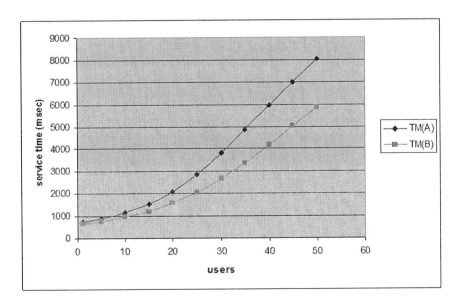

Figure 16. Service time prediction for the business process with TM_A or TM_B.

It should be noted that according to the results of the performability prediction, the candidate configuration containing the TM_A service is to be preferred, being the one that provides the best expected reward rate.

As aforementioned, the performability prediction leads to a choice of the initial configuration that does not correspond to what obtained by limiting the prediction to performance characteristics only.

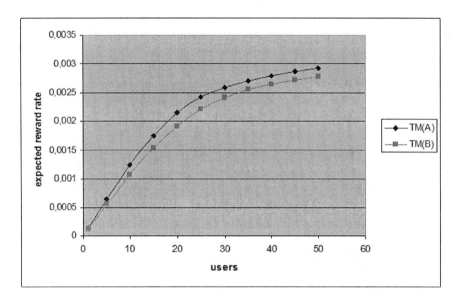

Figure 17. Expected reward rate for the business process with TM_A and TM_B.

CONCLUSIONS

This chapter has illustrated PyBPMN (Performability-enabled BPMN), a lightweight BPMN extension for the specification of properties that address the business process performability, a joint measure of the performance and reliability characteristics of a business process.

The chapter has also introduced a method that exploits PyBPMN to predict, at design time, the performability of a business process.

The proposed method, founded on a set of model transformations, yields as output the performability prediction by aggregating the results obtained from the separate prediction of performance and reliability properties. The proposed approach has been implemented into a prototype and applied to a simple but effective case study that has shown how the performability analysis may lead to predictions that do not correspond to those obtained by approaches that only take into account either the performance or the reliability attribute.

The proposed method has been applied at business process design time to identify the best initial configuration of the business process. Nevertheless, the degree of automation of the proposed method offers good potential for managing the performability of a business process along all lifecycle phases. In particular, on-going work includes the extension of the approach to the analysis of performability at execution time, in order to enable the performability-based dynamic reconfiguration of business processes.

REFERENCES

[1] G. Alonso, F. Casati, H. Kuno, V. Machiraju, *Web Services*, Springer-Verlag, 2004.

[2] J. Amsden *"Modeling with SoaML, the Service-Oriented Architecture Modeling Language"*. Technical article, IBM, 2010, http://www.ibm. com/developerworks/rational/library/09/modelingwithsoaml-1/index.html

[3] Apache ODE *(Orchestration Director Engine), http://ode.apache.org/*

[4] Becker J., Kugeler M., and Rosemann M., "Process Management. *A Guide for the Design of Business Processes"*. Springer-Verlag (2003).

[5] Bernardi, S., Merseguer, J., and Petriu, D. C. 2008. *Adding Dependability Analysis Capabilities to the MARTE Profile*. In Proceedings of the 11th international Conference on Model Driven Engineering Languages and Systems (Toulouse, France, September 28 - October 03, 2008). K. Czarnecki, I. Ober, J. Bruel, A. Uhl, and M. Völter, Eds. Lecture Notes In Computer Science, vol. 5301. Springer-Verlag, Berlin, Heidelberg, 736-750.

[6] Bernardi, S., Merseguer, J., Petriu, D.: *An UML profile for Dependability Analysis and Modeling of Software Systems*. Technical Report RR-08-05, Universidad de Zaragoza, Spain (2008) http://www.di.unito.it/bernardi/DAMreport08.pdf

[7] Bocciarelli P., D'Ambrogio A.: *Model-driven Performability Analysis of Composite Web Services. Model-driven Performability Analysis of Composite Web Services*. LNCS vol 5119/2008, Proceedings of the SPEC International Performance Evaluation Workshop (SIPEW 2008). Darmstadt, Germany, 27-28 June 2008.

[8] Bocciarelli P., D'Ambrogio A.: *A model-driven method for describing and predicting the reliability of composite services*. Software and

System Modeling, ISSN: 1619-1366, doi: 10.1007/s10270-010-0150-3. pp 1-16 (2010).

[9]   Cardoso J., Sheth A.P., Miller J.A., Arnold J. and Kochut K: *Quality of service for workflows and web service processes.* Journal of Web Semantics, 1(3), pp. 281-308 (2004)

[10] D'Ambrogio, A., Bocciarelli, P.: *A model-driven approach to describe and predict the performance of composite services.* In: WOSP 2007: Proceedings of the 6th international workshop on Software and performance, pp. 78–89. ACM Press, New York (2007)

[11] D'Ambrogio A., "*A Model-driven WSDL Extension for Describing the QoS of Web Services,*" Web Services, IEEE International Conference on, pp. 789-796, IEEE International Conference on Web Services (ICWS'06), 2006.

[12] D'Ambrogio A., *"A Model Transformation Framework for the Automated Building of Performance Models from UML Models".* In: Proceedings of the ACM Fifth International Workshop on Software and Performance (WOSP'05), Palma de Mallorca, Spain. (2005).

[13] Eclipse QVT Transformation Engine, *http://www.eclipse.org/m2m*

[14] G.P. Gu, D. Petriu, *"From UML to LQN by XML algebra-based model transformations".* In: Proceedings of the ACM Fifth International Workshop on Software and Performance (WOSP'05), Palma de Mallorca, Spain, (2005).

[15] Layered Queueing Network Solver software package *http://www .sce.carleton.ca/rads/lqns/*

[16] Leymann F.: *Web Services Flow Language*, Version 1.0, 2001

[17] Meyer J.F., *On evaluating performability of degradable computing systems, IEEE Transactions on Computers*, vol. C-29, no. 8, pp. 720-731, August 1980

[18] OASIS Web *Services Business Process Execution Language (WSBPEL),* version 2.0, http://docs.oasis-open.org/wsbpel/2.0/OS/wsbpel-v2.0-OS.html

[19] Object Management Group, *Business Process Modeling Notation (BPMN),* version 1.2, http://www.omg.org/spec/BPMN/1.2/

[20] Object Management Group, *Business Process Modeling Notation (BPMN),* RFP 2.0, http://www.bpmn.org/Documents/BPMN%202-0%20RFP%2007-06-05.pdf

[21] Object Management Group, *Business Process Modeling Notation (BPMN),* version 2.0 Beta 1, http://www.omg.org/spec/BPMN/2.0/ Beta1/PDF

[22] Object Management Group, *Business Process Modeling Notation (BPMN),* version 2.0 Beta 1, XMI Schema, bmi/09-05-04, http://www.omg.org/spec/BPMN/2.0/

[23] Object Management Group, *MDA Guide,* version 1.0.1

[24] Object Management Group, *XML Metadata Interchange (XMI) Specification,* version 2.1.1, December 2007.

[25] Object Management Group, *Meta Object Facility (MOF) Specification,* version 1.4

[26] Object Management Group, *Unified Modeling Language (UML) Specification,* version 2.2, February 2009.

[27] Object Management Group: *A UML profile for Modeling and Analysis of Real Time Embedded Systems,* v. 1.0, November 2009.

[28] Object Management Group: *Service oriented architecture Modeling Language,* v. 1.0 Beta 2, December 2009.

[29] Object Management Group: *Meta Object Facility (MOF) 2.0 Query/View/Transformation,* v1.0, April 2008.

[30] S. Oussena, B. *Barn, Layered process models: analysis and implementation (using MDA principles).* In: Cordeiro, Jose and Filipe, Joaquim, (ed.) ICEIS 2009: 11th International Conference on Enterprise Information Systems: proceedings. Institute for Systems and Technologies of Information, Control and Communication, pp. 168-175

[31] Ouyang C., Dumas M., Van der Aalst W. M., ter Hofstede A. H. and Mendling J., *"From business process models to process oriented software systems",* ACM Trans. Softw. Eng. Methodol. 19, 1 (Aug. 2009), pp 1-37.

[32] Ouyang C., Dumas M., ter Hofstede A. H. and der Aalst W. M., *Pattern-based translation of BPMN process models to BPEL services.* Int. J. Web Services Res. 5, 1, 42–61.

[33] C. Ouyang, W.M.P. van der Aalst, M. Dumas, and A.H.M. ter Hofstede. *From BPMN Process Models to BPEL Web Services.* In Proceedings of the 4th International Conference on Web Services (ICWS), Chicago IL, USA, pages 285-292. IEEE Computer Society, September 2006.

[34] M.P. Papazoglou, D. *Georgakopoulos, Service-oriented computing,* Communications of the ACM, vol. 46, no. 10, October 2003, pp. 25-28.

[35] Peltz C. (2003). *Web Services Orchestration and Choreography,* IEEE Computer, vol. 36, 2003, pp. 46-5

[36] Ko, R. K. 2009. *A computer scientist's introductory guide to business process management (BPM).* Crossroads 15, 4 (Jun. 2009), 11-18. DOI= http://doi.acm.org/10.1145/1558897.1558901

[37] Rosen, M. *BPM and SOA. Where does one end and the other begin?*
      http://www.bptrends.com/publicationfiles/01-
      06%20COL%20SOA%20where%20Does%20One%20End%20-
      %20Rosen.pdf
[38] Smith R. M., Trivedi Kishor S., Ramesh A. V.: *Performability Analysis:*
      Measures, an algorithm, and a Case Study. IEEE Transactions on
      Computers, 37(4): 406-417. (1988)
[39] Thatte S.: *XLANG Web Services for Business Process Design*, 2001.
[40] Whittaker, J.A. and Thomason, M.G.: *A Markov Chain Model for*
      Statistical Software Testing. IEEE Transactions on Software
      Engineering, 20 (10), pp. 812-824. (1994)
[41] Woodside C.M.: *Tutorial Introduction to Layered Modeling of Software*
      Performance - Edition 3.0, Department of Systems and Computer
      Engineering, Carleton University, Ottawa (Canada), May 2002.
[42] Xu, J., Oufimtsev, A., Woodside, M., and Murphy, L.: *Performance*
      modeling and prediction of enterprise JavaBeans with layered queuing
      network templates. ACM SIGSOFT Software Engineering. Notes.
      Volume 31. Issue 2 (2006).

In: Business Process Modeling
Editor: Jason A. Beckmann

ISBN: 978-1-61209-344-4

Chapter 2

CONCEPTUALIZING, ANALYZING AND COMMUNICATING THE BUSINESS MODEL

*Christian Nielsen**

Aalborg University, Fibigerstræde 4, 9220 Aalborg Ø. Denmark,

ABSTRACT

A business model is a sustainable way of doing business. Here sustainability stresses the ambition to survive even harsh business landscapes and create profits in the long run. Whether profits are retained by the shareholders or distributed in some degree to a broader mass of stakeholders is not the focus here. Rather, it is the point of this paper to illustrate how one may go about conceptualizing, analyzing and communicating the business model of a company. A business model describes the coherence in the strategic choices which makes possible the handling of the processes and relations which create value on both the operational, tactical and strategic levels in the organization. The business model is the platform which connects resources, processes and the supply of a service, which results in the fact that the company is profitable in the long term. Conceptualizing the business model is therefore concerned with identifying this platform, while analyzing it is concerned with gaining an understanding of precisely which levers of control are apt to deliver the value proposition of the company. Finally, communicating the

* Email: chn@business.aau.dk

business model is concerned with identifying the most important performance measures, both absolute and relative measures, and relating them to the overall value creation story.

Keywords: Business models, value creation story, value proposition, performance measurement

INTRODUCTION

A business model is a sustainable way of doing business. Here sustainability stresses the ambition to survive even harsh business landscapes and create profits in the long run. Whether profits are retained by the shareholders or distributed in some degree to a broader mass of stakeholders is not the focus here. Rather, it is the point of this paper to illustrate how one may go about conceptualizing, analyzing and communicating the business model of a company.

Sustainability is the propensity to survive and thus also the ability to stay competitive. As such, a business model cannot be a static way of doing business. It must be developed, nursed and optimized continuously in order for the company to meet changing competitive demands. Precisely how the company differentiates itself is the competitive strategy, whilst it is the business model that defines on which basis this is to be achieved; i.e. how it combines its know-how and resources to deliver the value proposition (which will secure profits and thus make the company sustainable).

In the last decades, the speed of change in the business landscape has continuously accelerated. In the late 1990's, the e-business revolution changed global competition, and during the early years of the new millennium the knowledge-based society along with rising globalization and the developments in the BRIC economies ensured that momentum continued upwards. According to Sweet (2001, 71) these changes in the business landscape and society have had major implications for firm-level demands such as how value is configured.

As new forms of value configurations emerge, so do new business models. Therefore, new analysis models that identify corporate resources such as knowledge and core processes are needed in order to illustrate the effects of decisions on value creation. Accordingly, managers as well as analysts must recognize that business models are made up of portfolios of different resources (also denoted assets) and not merely traditional physical and financial assets.

Therefore, "every company needs to create a business model that links combinations of assets to value creation" (Boulton, Libert, & Samek 1997, 33).

The rising interest in understanding and evaluating business models can to some extent be traced to the fact that new value configurations outcompete existing ways of doing business. There exist cases where some businesses are more profitable than others in the same industry, even though they apply the same strategy. This illustrates that a business model is different from a competitive strategy and a value chain. A value chain is a set of serially performed activities for a firm in a specific industry (Porter 1985). The difference thus lies in the way activities are performed (strategic and tactical choices), and therefore a business model is closely connected to the management control agenda.

The business model perspective has been found useful for aligning financial and non-financial performance measures with strategy and goals. In addition, communicative aspects from executive management to the rest of the organization, and also to external stakeholders such as bankers, investors and analysts, are also facilitated by a business model perspective.

Three empirical research projects inform the basis of the rest of this article:

1) A research project concerned with understanding the basics of the business model; characteristics and elements as well as tools for conceptualizing business models

2) A research project focusing on the analysis of the business model and the application of a series of analysis techniques

3) A research project focusing on the communication of business models

The rest of the paper is structured as follows: The following section introduces the business model concept and provides a helpful definition. The next section, 'Conceptualizing the business model', looks at which parameters and characteristics we need to understand in connection with the business model. In the section 'Analyzing the business model', the reader is introduced to the analytical guideline and the important aspects of relative and absolute business model evaluation, including the strengths of evaluation across time. In the section 'Communicating the business model', a series of cases and examples are presented, and the relationship between a business model description and an equity story is clarified. The article is concluded by a series of good advice on conceptualizing, analyzing and communicating the business model.

THE BUSINESS MODEL CONCEPT AND A DEFINITION

In the late 1990's, the 'business model' concept became almost synonymous with e-business and the emergence of the so-called new economy. The Internet had in essence created an array of new business models where the major focal point of the literature on business models from an e-business perspective became how to migrate successfully to profitable e-business models. See e.g. Hedman & Kalling (2001) for a comprehensive review. Therefore, much of the business model literature focusing on the e-business context concerns how such organizations can create value in comparison to their bricks and mortar counterparts (cf. Alt & Zimmermann 2001, Rappa 2001, Pigneur 2002).

However, far from all ways of doing business through the Internet have proven to be profitable, and accordingly there has been a substantial interest in explaining how the new distribution and communication channels form new business structures. One way of approaching this issue is through Amit & Zott's (2001) four dimensions of value-creation potential in e-businesses that have to be in place for an e-business model to be profitable: It must create efficiencies in comparison to existing ways of doing business (see also Farrell 2003, 107), and it must facilitate complementarities, novelty or enable the lock-in of customers (cf. Porter 2001, 68). For example, the creation of efficiencies is by DeYoung (2003) seen as the underlying notion of Internet based business models in the banking industry, while Gallaugher (2002) in general illustrates how e-commerce as a new distribution channel has created efficiencies, thus enabling new business models to emerge.

It should be noted that "[m]uch of what is being said about the New Economy is not that new at all. Waves of discontinuous change have occurred before", as Senge & Carstedt (2001, 24) state. Just think of how Henry Ford's business model revolutionized the car industry almost a century ago, or how Sam Walton revolutionized the retail industry in the 1960s with his information technology focus and choice of demographic attributes for store locations, thus creating an immense cost structure focus along with a monopolistic market situation.

According to Chesbrough & Rosenbloom (2002, 530), the origins of the business model concept can be traced back to Chandler's seminal book

'Strategy and Structure' from 1962. Strategy, Chandler states, "can be defined as the determination of the basic long-term goals and objectives of an enterprise, and the adoption of courses of action and the allocation of resources necessary for carrying out these goals" (1962, 13). Further developments in the concept travel through Ansoff's (1965) thoughts on corporate strategy to Andrews' (1980) definitions of corporate and business strategy, which, according to Chesbrough & Rosenbloom (2002), can be seen as a predecessor of and equivocated to that of a business model definition.

Child's (1972) paper on organizational structure, environment and performance, incidentally to a great extent influenced by Chandler's work, is, however, among the earliest to gather and present these thoughts diagrammatically. Although he does not explicitly refer to his schematization of "the role of strategic choice in a theory of organization" (Child 1972, 18) as a business model representation, the thoughts presented here incorporate many of the central elements presented within the recent literature on this emerging concept. For instance, Child's term 'prior ideology' covers the aspects of an organization's vision and value proposition, objectives, and strategy, while 'operating effectiveness' is viewed as an outcome of the organizational strategy and the elements: scale of operations, technology, structure, and human resources.

The recent research interest for new value configurations (Ramirez 1999; Stabell & Fjeldstad 1998; Sweet 2001) reflects a change in the competitive landscape towards more variety in value creation models within industries where previously the "name of the industry served as shortcut for the prevailing business model's approach to market structure" (Sandberg 2002, 3), competition now increasingly stands between competing business concepts (Hamel 2000). If firms within the same industry operate on the basis of different business models, different competencies and knowledge resources are key parts of the value creation, and mere benchmarking of intellectual capital indicators does not provide insight in the profit or growth potential of the firm. A comparison of the specific firm with its peer group requires interpretation based on an understanding of differences in business models.

If firms only disclose key performance indicators without disclosing the business model that explains the interconnectedness of the indicators and why the bundle of indicators is relevant for understanding the firms' strategy for value creation, this interpretation must be done by the analysts themselves. Currently, there exists no research based insight into how this reading and interpretation are conducted, and it is very likely that this understanding of firms' value creation would be facilitated if companies disclosed such information as an integral part of their strategy disclosure. From Nielsen (2005) the following definition of a business model is rendered:

> A business model describes the coherence in the strategic choices which makes possible the handling of the processes and relations which create value on both the operational, tactical and strategic levels in the organization. The business model is therefore the platform which connects resources, processes and the supply of a service which results in the fact that the company is profitable in the long term.

Conceptualizing the business model is therefore concerned with identifying this platform, while analyzing it is concerned with gaining an understanding of precisely which levers of control are apt to deliver the value proposition of the company. Finally, communicating the business model is concerned with identifying the most important performance measures, both absolute and relative measures, and relating them to the overall value creation story.

CONCEPTUALIZING THE BUSINESS MODEL

A business model is not merely a value chain, nor is it a corporate strategy. There exist many value configurations that are different to that of a value chain, like e.g. value networks and hubs (Stabell & Fjelstad 1998, Mintzberg & Van der Heyden 1999). Rather, a business model is concerned with the unique combination of attributes that deliver a certain value proposition. Therefore, a business model is the platform which enables the strategic choices to become profitable.

In some instances it can be difficult to distinguish between businesses that succeed because they are the best at executing a generic strategy and businesses that succeed because they have unique business models. This is an important distinction to make, and while some cases are clear-cut, others remain fuzzier.

One of the best examples of a business model that has changed an existing industry is Ryanair, which has essentially restructured the business model of the airline industry. As the air transport markets have matured, incumbent companies that have developed sophisticated and complex business models now face tremendous pressure to find less costly approaches that meet broad customer needs with minimal complexity in products and processes (Hansson et al. 2002).The generic strategy of Ryanair can be denoted as a low-price strategy. This option is open to all existing airlines, and many already compete on price. However, Ryanair was among the first airline companies to mould its business platform to create a sustainable low-price business. Many unique business models are easy to communicate because they have a unique quality about them; i.e. either a unique concept or value proposition. This is also the case for Ryanair. It is the "no-service business model". In fact, the business model is so well thought through that even the arrogance and attitude of the top management match the sleaziness and inconsideration of the rest of the business. But they can make money in an industry that has been under pressure for almost a decade, and for this they deserve recognition. Ryanair's business model narrative is the story of a novel flying experience. No other place in the world is it possible for humans to feel so much like livestock waiting for the butcher to arrive. It is only a shame that some of the customers are captive customers in the sense that they cannot afford to travel with an ordinary airline even if they wanted to.

A much applied example in the management literature is Toyota. However, Toyota did not really change the value proposition of the car industry. They were able to achieve superior quality through JIT and Lean management technologies, and they may have made slightly smaller cars than the American car producers, but their value proposition and operating platform were otherwise unchanged. The same can be said for Ford in the early 20th century. Ford's business setup was not really a new business model. It sold one car model in one colour, but so did others at the time. Ford was able to reduce costs through a unique organization of the production setup, but the value proposition was not unique.

In the 1990's, Dell changed the personal computer industry by applying the Internet as a novel distribution channel. This platform as a foundation of the pricing strategy took out several parts of the sales channel, leaving a larger cut to Dell and cheaper personal computers to the customers. Nowadays this distribution strategy is not a unique business model anymore as many other laptop producers apply it. Therefore, it is also a good example of the fact that what is unique today is not necessarily unique tomorrow.

According to Hamel & Skarzynski (2001), innovation is an important mechanism with respect to ensuring wealth creation, but it is also a prerequisite for sustainable development because "today's competitive advantage becomes tomorrow's albatross", as Christensen (2001, 105) expresses it. Having the right business model at the present does not necessarily guarantee success for years on end (Linder & Cantrell 2001) as new technology or changes in the business environment and customer base can influence profitability (Delmar 2003). The point to be made here is that if the value proposition is not affected in some manner, then it is most likely not a new business model. However, it could be the case that the value proposition is not affected, but the business' value generating attributes are radically different from those of the competitors. Three examples of this are:

1) The value proposition of two companies producing kitchen appliances. One may be more high-end than the other, but this is a part of the competitive strategy, not the actual business model

2) The value proposition of two companies producing laptops. One may be priced lower because the range is smaller and the design kept to one colour etc. This is not equivalent to different business models, but also a question of competitive strategy and customer selection. However, if one of the producers decides to alter the traditional distribution model, cutting out store placement and setting up technical support as local franchisees only, that could be a new business model

3) Two hair salons will both be performing haircuts, but their value propositions may be vastly different according to the physical setup around the core attribute

Which Parameters do we need to Understand?

Remembering that the business model is the platform which enables the strategic choices to become profitable, then it is clear that a business model is not a pricing strategy, a new distribution channel, an information technology, nor is it a quality control scheme in the production setup. A business model is concerned with the value proposition of the company, but it is not the value proposition alone as it in itself is supported by a number of parameters and characteristics. The question is here: how is the strategy and value proposition of the company leveraged?

To understand the foundations of the business model, metaphorically speaking, the pillars on which the platform rests, it is necessary to look at the organizational attributes of the company. In doing so, the focus should not be on the elements themselves, i.e. organizational structure, alliances, management processes, customer types, but rather on the characteristics of the links between them. A model that provides a good overview of the elements which need to be taken into account when conceptualizing the business model is provided by KPMG's Strategic-Systems Auditing (SSA) framework (Bell et al. 1997).

Bell & Solomon define the business model as: "a simplified representation of the network of causes and effects that determine the extent to which the entity creates value and earns profits" (2002, xi). Compared to the suggestions by Bell et al. (1997), the recent framework focuses more narrowly on value creation and has predominately internal focus incorporating the elements of value drivers, value creation, and representation. As a distinctive feature, the SSA model departs from an auditing perspective where Bell et al. (1997) argue for the importance of gaining an understanding of the client's strategic advantage. This is, however, not only a necessity from an auditing perspective since understanding a company's strategic advantage is the prerequisite for understanding how it creates value.

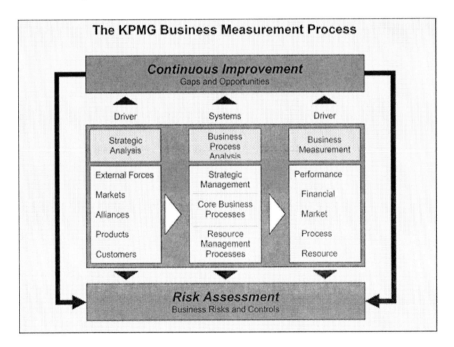

Figure 1. The KPMG Business Measurement Process.

Gaining an understanding of key value creation processes and related competencies that enable the company to realize its strategy is an essential element of such an analysis. By measuring and benchmarking the performance of core business, management and support processes, the 'KPMG Business Measurement Process', depicted in figure 4, facilitates and enhances an understanding of the risks that threaten the attainment of the company's business objectives. The following of this framework is argued to lead to an understanding of the client's business model and a documentation of the company's ability to create value and generate future cash flows through depiction of the company's specific process analyses, key performance indicators, and business risk profile. Thus, a similar procedure could potentially form the foundation for external communication more generally.

The SSA model is based on an analysis procedure that departs in the strategic analysis of the external forces affecting the company and the markets on which it operates, along with an analysis of its alliances, products, and customers. Next, an analysis of the business processes regarding strategic management processes, core business processes, and resource management processes leads to a so-called Entity Level Business Model and the identification of key business performance measures.

SSA gives an idea of the parameters that make up and define the outskirts of a business model. Through the strategic analysis, the following aspects of the organization are described: external forces, markets, alliances, products, and customers. Next, the SSA model includes a process analysis tool which helps the analyst from a risk based perspective to find the most appropriate KPI's and controls of key risks for the company to be able to deliver the value proposition and through this identify the characteristics and key aspects of the links between organizational elements. The business process analysis is applied on three archetypes of processes, namely: strategic management processes, core business processes, and resource management processes. Finally, the first two steps lead to the actual business performance measurement including the identification of performance KPI's according to the four dimensions: financial, market, process, and resource.

Another more recent contribution to the field of business model conceptualization is Osterwalder et al. (2010). Here the value proposition links the company's infrastructure (down-stream activities and management to execution) with the customer (distribution and after sales relationships). In comparison to Bell et al. (1997), Osterwalder et al. (2010) get somewhat closer to the goal of identifying the 'how' of the business model because they place the value proposition at the centre of the model as an aligning feature between infrastructure interrelations such as competences, partner network and value configuration, and customer interrelations such as customer relationships, distribution channel, and target customers.

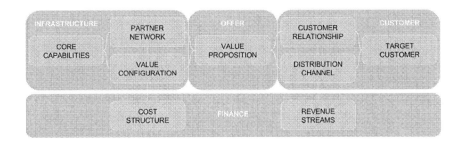

Figure 2. Business model design template (Osterwalder et al. 2010).

Despite these developments, the ideas put forth here come short of illustrating how the specific linkages of value creation work. In addition, this proposal fails to identify that external forces such as the economy, policy, consumer sentiment and NGO's also affect the ability to deliver the company's value proposition.

The two models described above illustrate two different ways of approaching the generic parameters of a business model. Together they provide a good overview of the elements that may affect the uniqueness of a business model. However, both models have weaknesses when it comes to highlighting the platform for success. How to avoid this will be illustrated in the analysis and communication sections below in this article.

ANALYZING THE BUSINESS MODEL

In the section above, it became evident that a business model potentially consists of the interaction between many different parameters of the organization. Some unique business models thus involve extremely complex interdependencies, whereas, in other cases, it can be extremely simple to understand the specifics of a business model. An example of a company where a complex set of interdependencies create a unique business model is the Danish medico-technology company, Coloplast. For Coloplast the platform for a long-term sustainable business rests on the interaction between the ability to integrate the ideas and requests of the decision-making nurse-groups into product development without renouncing the product quality perceptions of end-users. Measuring the performance and development of these interdependencies is extremely complex. An example of an easy to understand business model is Ryanair's: "a ticket includes no service whatsoever. If you require any extras or have physical handicaps, then remember your credit card".

The notion put forth here is that if it is difficult for the company to conceptualize the business model, then it may be even more difficult for external parties to analyze it. At present there exists very little literature on the aspects of analyzing business models. However, several management and performance measurement models can be mobilized to some extent in the understanding of business model performance. Below, four perspectives of analysis are identified, each with differing ambitions and therefore also with different theoretical underpinnings, namely: processes, causality, quality and competences.

It is widely accepted that intellectual capital, strategy and other drivers of value creation constitute strategically important elements for the future profitability and survival of companies. Many firms already disclose much supplementary information in their management commentary regarding strategy, market competition, technological developments and products in the pipeline. Also, in the Nordic countries and more recently in a number of other European countries, companies have been experimenting with disclosing such voluntary and forward-looking disclosures through intellectual capital statements.

The problem - as well as the prospect - with strategy is that it is about being different. Hence, the bundle of indicators on strategy, intellectual capital etc. that will be relevant to disclose will differ among firms. For such information to make any sense at all, it should be communicated in the firm's strategic context as this would show its relevance in relation to the company's value creation process. In other words, it does not make sense to insert such information into a standardized accounting regime.

The SSA framework applies a risk-based perspective on value creation and combines the analysis of strategic and business related processes with risks and risk-controls to the identification of key performance indicators (KPI's). Thus, the process analysis template of the SSA framework helps the analyst to conceive how the underlying aspects of performance are related to each other via a risk-based approach.

The Balanced Scorecard's strategy map analysis is another methodology that helps to integrate KPI's and illustrates their interconnectedness. The Balanced Scorecard takes its point of departure in a cause-and-effect approach on competitive strategy. The strategy map methodology helps the analyst to link KPI's through the four perspectives of the Balanced Scorecard. The Business Excellence model is a quality-based perspective to identifying KPI's.

Unlike the Balanced Scorecard, the Business Excellence model does not assume causal links, but rather a milder form of relatedness between measures.

In the section below, a fourth model for the analysis of performance measures is applied. It is a model developed for the analysis of the intellectual capital value proposition by Mouritsen et al. (2003). In its original presentation, the model was proposed to help create a set of rules for the analysis of intellectual capital statements that allowed the reader to appreciate the content of an intellectual statement in such a way that he or she could make an independent judgment of it. Later, it has been proven applicable to the analysis of many types of strategy-related disclosures, including voluntary CSR-reports, IPO prospectuses as well as the management review sections of traditional financial reports.

The Analytical Guideline

The idea of the analytical guideline was to develop analytical rules for voluntary information which paralleled the analytical concerns of the financial statement. According to Bukh et al. (2005) insight into financial assets could be translated to insight into the constellation of knowledge and value creation resources; insight about investments could be translated into insight about upgrading competences and resources; and finally, insight into performance could be translated into insight about the effects of knowledge, innovation and strategic choices.

The information 'input' for the analytical model can be derived from the information channels of the company which is to be analyzed; e.g. from the annual report, corporate website, management interviews or reports of financial analysts. In the case where an annual report is the supplier of information, the input thus becomes the specific indicators representing value creation, management challenges and the activities that the company performs. The indicators are disentangled from the text of the annual report through the analytical model that organises the indicators according to three general problematisations of the firm (similar to the problematisations of the financial statement): What is the composition of value creation resources (what is the composition of assets)? What are the activities made to upgrade competences and resources (which investments are made in the firm)? What are the effects of knowledge, innovation and strategic choices (what is profitability)? These questions are concerned with the assessment of the firm's business model.

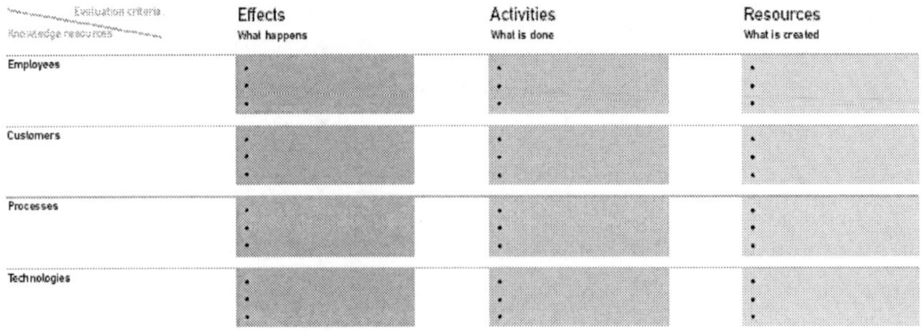

Evaluation criteria / Knowledge resources	Effects What happens	Activities What is done	Resources What is created
Employees			
Customers			
Processes			
Technologies			

Figure 3. The analytical model (Mouritsen et al. 2003b).

Unlike an accounting system, the analysis model is *not* an input/output-model. There is no perception that any causal links between actions exist to develop employees and the effect in that area – e.g. increased employee satisfaction. The effect of such an action may appear as a customer effect: The employee becomes more qualified and capable of serving the customers better. The task of the analysis is thus to explain these 'many-to-many relations' in the model. The classification itself does not explain the relations, just as increased expenses for R&D alone do not lead to increased turnover in the financial accounting system.

From Bukh et al. (2005) the assessment criteria of the analysis model based on indicators attached to the three main questions of the analysis are illustrated:

Resource indicators concern the portfolio of the company's resources, i.e. the company's stock and composition of resources within the areas of employees, customers, processes and technologies, and illustrate a starting point from which action can be taken. The indicators deal with relatively stable units such as e.g. 'a customer', 'an employee', 'a computer', 'a process' etc. They answer questions such as 'how many?' and 'which share?' and thus illustrate how big, how varied, how complex and how correlated the resources are. The managerial actions related to these resources are portfolio decisions; i.e. decisions on how many of the different types of knowledge resources the company wants.

Activity indicators describe the company's activities to upgrade its resources; i.e. activities initiated to upgrade, strengthen or develop its resource portfolio. The indicators illustrate the direction in which the organization is working and help to answer the question 'What is being done?'; e.g. what does the company do to develop and improve its knowledge resources through e.g. continuing education, investments in processes, activities to educate or attract customers, presentations etc. The attached management actions are thus upgrading activities.

Effect indicators reflect the consequences or the total effects of the company's development and use of resources. As with an accounting system, the model only shows the effects; it does not seek to explain from where they arise. The analyst may seek such explanations on the basis of the model, but not within the model itself. These indicators help us to establish whether we are arriving where we expected to.

Thus, when analyzing the interrelations of the business model it is possible to apply the ideas of a strategic narrative. Like all other stories, this narrative has a beginning, an action and an ending. So does the strategic narrative, It has resources, activities and effects. Together with an understanding of the company's strategy and the key management challenges facing the executive management, it is possible to mobilize the questions of analysis illustrated above to identify the key indicators of the business model. Evaluating the business model can therefore be done in a series of steps.

A first step could be to evaluate the identified indicators in a scorecard-like fashion in relation to a set of expected targets for each indicator. Thereafter the indicators can be evaluated in the analysis model by asking which indicators affect each other. This analysis can be completed by asking whether some of the 12 boxes have missing indicators. Together with the indicators at hand, management should ask themselves how they fit into the story of what the company does and how it is unique. In this manner, management is gradually moving closer to its business model narrative supported by performance measures. In order to assess if the composition, structure and use of the company resources are appropriate, it is necessary to consider the development of the indicators over time, and finally the company may pursue relative and absolute measures for benchmarking across time and across competitors.

COMMUNICATING THE BUSINESS MODEL

The point of departure for many of the recent developments in voluntary reporting, especially the so-called narrative models, is to illustrate the flows of value creation by linking indicators to strategy and supporting an understanding of them by providing a context giving narrative (Nielsen, Roslender & Bukh 2009). Mouritsen and Larsen (2005) label this a process of "entangling" the indicators, arguing that individual pieces of information and measurements by themselves can be difficult to relate to any conception of value creation. As such, this "flow" approach is concerned with identifying which knowledge resources drive value creation instead of assigning a specific dollar value to those resources (Bukh 2002).

Hägglund (2001) and Mouritsen et al. (2001) accentuate that the understanding of the firm's value creation would be facilitated if companies disclosed their value drivers as an integral part of the strategy disclosure in the management review. Further, this communication would be even more effective if the framework for disclosure was based on a common understanding of the company's value drivers (Bukh & Johanson 2003, Osterwalder 2004). Along these lines, Bukh (2002) and Kozberg (2001) suggest that the business model can enable the creation of a comprehensive and more correct set of non-financial value drivers of the company, thereby constituting a useful reference model for disclosure.

The problem with trying to visualize the company's "business model" is that it very quickly becomes a generic organization diagram illustrating the process of transforming inputs to outputs in a chain-like fashion. The reader is thus more often than not left wondering where the focus is in the organization, and key differentiating aspects of the business model are drowned in attempts to illustrate the whole business. This is why the communicative aspects are so important.

From a narrative perspective, business models can be a support mechanism for projection of management's view to the organization through e.g. storytelling. The organizational narrative is also a kind of abbreviation supporting the ability of remote control, in essence constituting a representation of the business through a description; i.e. a story of how it works (Magretta 2002b) and the relationships it is engaged in. Very much in line with Hamel's (2000) ideas, Morris (2003) conceptualizes the business model as a "comprehensive description of the business". A business model, according to Morris, is therefore a description of the system, including how the experiences of creating and delivering value may evolve along with the changing needs and preferences of customers (Morris 2003, 17). As Sandberg states, "business models describe and explain" (2002, 4), and Magretta argues that business models are merely "stories that explain how enterprises work" (2002a, 4). Such a narrative is an explanation of how the organization intends to implement its value proposition, much like the function of the knowledge narrative of an intellectual capital statement (Mouritsen et al. 2003a).

The business model may potentially constitute a platform for the company's supplementary reporting (cf. Nielsen & Bukh 2011), for example, concerning strategy, value creation processes, knowledge resources etc. Generally seen, it is about communicating the company's strategy, critical success factors, degree of risk, market conditions etc. in such a way that the investors realistically can assess how the company is actually doing and which expectations they may have to the future development. In practice, it has proven fairly difficult to do this in a way which is not too comprehensive and complicated, and which does not in an inappropriate way go too close to information which cannot be published, e.g. for the sake of legal requirements, partners or competitive conditions.

Internationally, several committees, commissions and groups of experts have during the past ten years worked on the development of guidelines and recommendations. For example, Blair & Wallman (2001, 59) have argued that the company's supplemental reporting should reflect the dynamics which drive the company's value creation. The company's communication and reporting should ultimately constitute a representation of the company's business model "by describing the relationships among the various input measures and outcome measures, and to link the primary inputs to intermediate inputs and, ultimately, to financial performance and other measures of total value creation" (Blair & Wallman 2001, 43).

In relation to the communication and Investor Relations work, the business model may thus be perceived as a model which helps the company's management to communicate and share their understanding of the company's business logic with external stakeholders (Fensel 2001). This is often described as "equity story" in finance circles. These stakeholders do not only comprise analysts and investors, but also partners, the society and potential employees. This business model-bound equity story is related to the business-oriented tendencies within corporate branding, which for example Hatch and Schultz (2003) are exponents for. The main point here is that corporate branding is about rendering visible the interaction between the company's strategy, internal company culture and image. Thus, corporate branding is an interconnected practice for the whole organization and not only an expression of the marketing department's perspective. In this way, the notion branding becomes a question of explaining how the company earns money rather than an explanation of responsibility towards internal and external stakeholders.

The idea of equity story communication is thus that the uniqueness of the company's value creation is taken as the starting point in relation to external parties. Sandberg (2002) formulates this in the following way: "Spell out how your business is different from all the others." Osterwalder & Pigneur (2003) consider the process which the management is going through in connection with a modelling of the company as an important tool to identify and understand central elements and relations in the business, for example value drivers and other causal relations.

Together with consistency, a firm structure for the communication of information and the very information may help the company's external stakeholders to understand how new events affect its future prospects. In this way, the company can minimise the spread in the analysts' estimates which affect the uncertainty about the "real" price determination which, as discussed above, affects the capital costs.

GOOD ADVICE ON CONCEPTUALIZING, ANALYZING AND COMMUNICATING THE BUSINESS MODEL

On the basis of the discussions above and a recent research project covering the communicative and analytical aspects of business models, ten pieces of advice for the successful explanation of the business model have been prepared. These guidelines express what is believed to be the easiest way of explaining and communicating a business model in practice.

1. Describe the Strategy Platform

A business model describes the platform by which the company puts its strategy into practice. This platform may differ significantly between companies. In the case of Danske Bank, the IT platform is the key that enables a smooth M&A. In Coloplast, the customer feedback platform is leading the company to innovative products. B&O's products are based on a design-, functionality- and lifestyle-platform. In A.P. Møller, it is their cultural and financial platform that makes the company unique. And Bavarian Nordic's technological platform may in time blaze the trail for new market segments.

The business model framework provides the companies with a tool to structure their information and communication – their supplementary report/management review/non-financial reporting and the investor site on the company's homepage.

2. Create a Connecting Story of Value Creation

It is crucial for the readers' understanding of the business model that the company presents a coherent picture of the company's value creation; e.g. by providing an insight into the interrelations that induce value creation in the company. Moreover, the non-financial reporting should follow up on the strategy plans and development in the business model in order to ensure consistency over time. A business model can be seen as a regression of the company's value creating elements, where the elasticities belonging to the identified variables are explained in words or by figures, and where the connections between the value creating elements are explained. However, a business model should not necessarily be understood as a value chain, and it should therefore not necessarily be reported as one. An alternative way of looking at the business model is through the so-called onion metaphor. Here, we start by describing the core, namely the company's cash flow, and then we move outwards through the different layers of the company. The further away from the core (cash flow), the better view of the size of the onion we get. We will fairly quickly be informed of the most important aspects of the company's value creation, and we may stop when we feel that we have gained sufficient knowledge about the company

3. Focus on the Connections and the Interrelations

The core of a business model description is the connections between the different elements that we traditionally divide the management review into. Companies often report a lot of information about e.g. customer relations, employee competencies, knowledge sharing, innovation and risks, but this information may seem unimportant if the company fails to show how the various elements of the value creation interrelate and which changes we should keep an eye on.

4. Be Explicit about the Organisation's Whereabouts in the Value Chain

Place the company in the industrial value chain and use this as a basis for comparing the company with its closest competitors. What are the advantages of the different ways of controlling resources and customers both upstream and downstream in the value chain? An example of this could be a comparison of LM Glasfiber and Vestas' different perspectives on the value chain in the wind energy sector, or DLH's approach to import of wood.

5. Avoid Empty Expressions and Buzz-Words

Avoid empty expressions such as: "We are innovative". What is really interesting is why and how the company is innovative. The reader wants to know in what way the company differs from its competitors. Other empty expressions could be: "We want to be market leaders" and "knowledge is our greatest asset". Furthermore, it is important to avoid buzz words, especially if the company has many private investors.

6. Be aware that Transparency has Different Meanings

Transparency means being able to see through and in relation to the business model, it is more precisely concerned with the ability to explain the different aspects of value creation across the value chain, and how these aspects affect the company's bottom line. However, it is important to note that transparency varies according to the time horizon. In the short term, creating transparency is concerned with accessibility and news flow, whereas in the long term, transparency is concerned with creating an understanding of strategy, access to resources and market developments. Transparency also differs between private and institutional investors. For private investors, transparency is about creating a simplified understanding of the company's concept. For institutional investors, transparency is about filtering and structuring the massive amounts of information available for their decision-making. In both instances, the company's business model is a good point of departure.

7. The Broad Information Channels have the Highest Influence on Transparency

The wide information channels still have the greatest influence on transparency. Communication via the company's homepage thus proved to have the most significant influence on transparency. The paramount factor correlating with the use of homepages was the size of the company. Thus, large companies use homepages to a much larger extent than small companies, which is quite a paradox since the internet is one of the cheapest ways to mass-communicate with the capital market.

8. Use the Spread in Consensus Estimates as a Measure of IR Success

Use the spread in consensus estimates as a useful indicator when the company is followed by more than five analysts. There is a positive, significant correlation between the company's IR activities and the consensus estimates for the coming year. This could indicate that if the company intensifies its IR activities, then the standard deviation for the consensus estimates will grow. This may be due to information overload.

Consensus estimates with a time horizon beyond one year will give a negative correlation. This means that companies with higher information levels may have lower standard deviation levels in the long term. The information that is conveyed through IR is of a more strategic and market-oriented type and therefore concerns the long-term perspective. Companies with a large amount of shares tied in strategic investments, i.e. less free float, had a higher level of information. This result is quite interesting since companies with a large free float typically are associated with high levels of information.

9. Explain the Business Model as a Forward Oriented Statement

A business model is a forward-looking statement which goes beyond an identification of the company's immediate cash flows. In capital market language, one would say: It is a statement on how the company will survive longer than till the end of the budget period. This means that when describing one´s business model, it is not enough to talk about the company's historic development, not even if it includes an account of the company's historic value creation, the company's concept and how the company's objectives and strategy have turned out.

10. Establish Trust in the Communication through the use of Performance Measures

Another central tool when describing a company's history is to support facts by non-financial performance measures. One thing is to state that one's business model is based on mobilizing customer feedback in the innovation process, another thing is to explain by what means this will be done, and even more demanding is proving the effort by indicating: 1) how many resources the company devotes to this effort; 2) how active the company is in this matter, and whether it stays as focussed on the matter as initially announced; and 3) whether the effort has had any effect, e.g. on customer satisfaction, innovation output etc.

CONCLUSION

Disclosure of information on strategies, business models, critical success factors, risk factors and value drivers in general has gained importance in recent years. Policy makers and academics have argued that the demand for external communication of new types of value drivers is rising as companies increasingly base their competitive strengths and thus the value of the company on know-how, patents, skilled employees and other intangibles.

In parallel with the focus on disclosure of value drivers, the concept of business models has also gained popularity. However, business models in terms of "ways of doing business" have always existed. The business model reflects the company's way of competing, whether it concerns being unique or being the most cost-efficient company in the industry. The supply of information on firms' value creating processes and value drivers has actually been increasing in various reporting media such as annual reports, IPO prospectuses and the reports of financial analysts. Furthermore, some firms, especially in the Nordic countries, have started developing Intellectual Capital (IC) reports that communicate how knowledge resources are managed in the firms within a strategic framework, and new models for reporting on stakeholder value creation and CSR are gradually emerging. Despite this, an explicit recognition of value creation as a central part of a business model is generally lacking in this literature.

It is also noticeable that even though disclosure of information from companies has been increasing, there are no clear signs that the particular information demands of investors and analysts have been met. The paradox is therefore that while there are well-developed arguments for disclosure and evidence indicates that companies are disclosing more and more information, there are also indications that disclosure is insufficient. This leads us to consider whether we, as often stated, are facing a reporting gap, or rather an understanding gap. This is where the business model can be applied.

REFERENCES

Alt, R., & H.-D. Zimmermann 2001. *Preface: Introduction to Special Section – Business Models,* Electronic Markets, Vol. 11, No. 1, pp. 1-7.

Amit, R. & C. Zott 2001. *Value Creation in e-business, Strategic Management* Journal, Vol. 22, pp. 493–520.

Ansoff, I. 1965. Corporate Strategy. McGraw-Hill.

Bell, T. & I. Solomon 2002. *Cases in Strategic-Systems Auditing.* KPMG LLP.

Bell, T., F. Marrs, I. Solomon & H. Thomas 1997. *Auditing Organizations Through a Strategic-Systems Lens: The KPMG Business Measurement Process.* KPMG LLP.

Blair, M. & S. Wallman 2001. *Unseen Wealth.* Brookings Institution, Washington D.C.

Boulton, R.E.S., B.D. Libert & S.M. Samek. 1997. *Cracking the Value Code: How successful businesses are creating wealth in the New Economy,* New York: Harper Collins Publishers.

Bukh, P.N. & U. Johanson. 2003. *Research and knowledge interactions: Guidelines for IC reporting.* Journal of Intellectual Capital, Vol. 4, No. 4, pp. 576-587.

Bukh, P.N. 2002. *Disclosure of intellectual capital – Indicators or models? A matter of accounting or strategy.* Working Paper, Aarhus School of Business.

Bukh, P.N., C. Nielsen, P. Gormsen & J. Mouritsen. 2005. *Disclosure of Information on Intellectual Capital indicators in Danish IPO Prospectuses.* Accounting, Auditing & Accountability Journal, Vol. 18, No. 6, pp. 713-732.

Chandler, A.D., Jr. 1962. *Strategy and Structure: Chapters in the History of the Industrial Enterprise.* Cambridge: The M.I.T. Press.

Chesbrough, H. & R.S. Rosenbloom 2002. *The role of the business model in capturing value from innovation: Evidence from Xerox Corporation's spin-off companies,* Industrial and Corporate Change, Vol. 11, No. 3, pp. 529-555.

Child, J. 1972. *Organizational Structure, Environment and Performance: The Role of Strategic Choice,* Sociology, Vol. 6, pp. 1-22.

Christensen, C.M. 2001. *The Past and Future of Competitive Advantage,* MIT Sloan Management Review, Vol. 42, No. 2, pp. 105-109.

Delmar, D.R. 2003. *The Rise of the CSO,* Journal of Business Strategy, March/April, pp. 8-10.

DeYoung, R. 2003. *The Performance of Internet-based Business Models: Evidence from the Banking Industry,* Journal of Business.

Farrell, D. 2003. *The Real New Economy,* Harvard Business Review, Vol. 81, No. 10, pp. 105-113.

Fensel, D. (2001). *Ontologies: Silver Bullet for Knowledge Management and Electronic commerce.* Heidelberg: Springer-Verlag.

Gallaugher, J.M. 2002. *E-Commerce and the Undulating Distribution Channel,* Communications of the Association for Computing Machinery, Vol. 45, No. 7, pp. 89-95.

Hamel, G. & Skarzynski 2001. *Innovation: The New Route to Wealth,* Journal of Accountancy, November, pp. 65-68.

Hamel, G. 2000. *Leading the revolution.* Boston: Harvard Business School Press.

Hansson, T., J. Ringbeck & M. Franke. 2002. *Flight for Survival: A New Business Model for the Airline Industry,* Strategy + Business, Vol. 31.

Hatch, M.J. & M. Schultz, 2003, *Bringing the corporation into corporate branding,* European Journal of Marketing, Vol. 37 Iss: 7/8, pp.1041 – 1064.

Hedman, J. & T. Kalling (2001). *The business model: a mean to understand the business context of information and communication technology.* Working paper 2001/9, Institute of Economic Research, School of Economics and Management, Lund Universitet.

Hägglund, P.B. 2001. *Företaget som investeringsobjekt – Hur placerare och analytiker arbetar med att ta fram ett investeringsobjekt.* Akademisk avhandling för avläggende av ekonomie doktorsexamen vid Handleshögskolen i Stockholm.

Kozberg, A. 2001. *The Value Drivers of Internet Stocks: A Business Models Approach,* Working paper, Zicklin School of Business, CUNY – Baruch College.

Linder, J. & S. Cantrell 2002. *What makes a good business model anyway? Can yours stand the test of change?* Outlook, www.accenture.com

Magretta, J. 2002a. *Why business models matter.* Harvard Business Review, May, pp. 3-8.

Magretta, J. 2002b. *What Management Is: How it Works and why it's Everyone's Business.* The Free Press: New York.

Mintzberg, H. & L. Van der Heyden. 1999. *Organigraphs: Drawing how Companies Really Work,* Harvard Business Review, September – October, pp. 87-94.

Morris, L. 2003. Business Model Warfare: *The Strategy of Business Breakthroughs,* InnovationLabs White Paper, prepared & published jointly with A-CASA.

Mouritsen, J., H. T. Larsen and P.N. Bukh. 2001. *Intellectual Capital and the 'Capable Firm': Narrating, Visualising and Numbering for Managing Knowledge.* Accounting, Organisations and Society 26(7):735-762.

Mouritsen, J., Bukh, P.N, Flagstad, K., Thorbjørnsen, S., Johansen, M.R., Kotnis, S., Larsen, H.T., Nielsen, C., Kjærgaard, I., Krag, L., Jeppesen, G., Haisler, J. & Stakemann, B. (2003*). Intellectual Capital Statements – The New Guideline Copenhagen: Danish Ministry of Science, Technology and Innovation.* (www.vtu.dk/icaccounts)

Mouritsen, J., Bukh, P.N, Johansen, M.R., Larsen, H.T., Nielsen, C., Haisler, J. & Stakemann, B. 2003. *Analysing Intellectual Capital Statements. Danish Ministry of Science, Technology and Innovation,* Copenhagen. (www.vtu.dk/icaccounts).

Mouritsen, J. & Larsen, H.T.. (2005). *The 2nd wave of knowledge management: The management control of knowledge resources through intellectual capital information,* Management Accounting Research, 16(4), 371-394.

Nielsen, C., R. Roslender & P.N. Bukh 2009. *Intellectual Capital Reporting: Can a strategy perspective solve accounting problems?* In Lytras & Ordonez de Pablos (Eds.) Knowledge Ecology in Global Business, IGI Global.

Nielsen, C. & P.N. Bukh. 2011. *What constitutes a Business Model: The perception of financial analysts.* Accepted for publication in International Journal of Learning and Intellectual Capital.

Nielsen, C. 2005. *Comments on the IASB discussion paper concerning Management   Commentary.* (http://www.iasb.org/current/comment_letters.asp)

Osterwalder, A. & Y. Pigneur. 2003. *Towards Business and Information Systems Fit through a Business Model Ontology.* Working paper, Ecole des HEC, University of Lausanne.

Osterwalder, A. 2004. *The Business Model Ontology: A Proposition in a Design Science Approach.* PhD thesis University of Lausanne.

Osterwalder, A., Y. Pigneur, A. *Smith, and 470 practitioners from 45 countries,* 2010, Business Model Generation, self published.

Pigneur, Y. 2002. *A framework for defining e-business models.* Working paper, Ecole des HEC, University of Lausanne.

Porter, M.E. 1985. *Competitive Advantage.* New York: The Free Press.

Porter, M.E. 2001, *Strategy and the Internet, Harvard Business Review,* March, pp.Ramirez 1999;

Rappa, M. 2001. *Managing the digital enterprise - Business Models on the Web,* http://ecommerce.ncsu.edu/business_models.html

Sandberg, K.D. 2002. *Is it time to trade in your business model?* Harvard Management Update, January, pp. 3-5.

Senge, P.M & G. Carstedt 2001. *Innovating Our Way to the Next Industrial Revolution, MIT Sloan Management Review,* Winter, pp. 24-38.

Stabell, C.B. & Ø. D. Fjeldstad 1998. *Configuring value for competitive advantage: On chains, shops and networks.* Strategic Management Journal, Vol. 19, pp. 413–437.

Sweet, 2001. *Strategic value configuration logics and the 'new' economy: a service economy revolution?* International Journal of Service Industry Management, Vol. 12, No.1, pp.70-83.

In: Business Process Modeling ISBN: 978-1-61209-344-4
Editor: Jason A. Beckmann ©2011 Nova Science Publishers, Inc.

Chapter 3

BUSINESS PROCESS MODELING AND AUTOMATION WITH GENERAL AND DOMAIN SPECIFIC LANGUAGES

Anca Daniela Ionita[1], and Jacky Estublier[2],†*

[1]Automatic Control and Computers Faculty, University "Politehnica" of Bucharest, Spl.Independentei 313, 060042, Bucharest, Romania
[2]LIG-IMAG, 220, rue de la Chimie BP5338041 Grenoble Cedex 9, France

ABSTRACT

The role of business process models, as models in general, has been considerably changed from describing scenarios (contemplative models) towards actual coordinating activity execution (productive models) and from technical expert privilege to domain expert routine task.

Therefore, the challenge today is to reconcile two requirements: i) provide high level formalisms to domain experts, for the definition of models, and ii) execute these models, by mapping the abstract activities on various pieces of code and implementation artifacts. Automation of business processes, which is a pillar of nowadays frameworks evolvability, requires filling the gap between high level formalisms and execution. How this is performed is the topic of our chapter, which analyzes two approaches: the former based on large, general modeling

---

* E-mail address: Anca.Ionita @ aii.pub.ro
† E-mail address: Jacky.Estublier @ imag.fr

languages, adopted as standards, and the latter based on small and composable domain specific languages. Examples of architectures driven by these process languages are presented, and solutions applied for the necessary transformations between different layers of abstraction are described.

1. INTRODUCTION

Many systems incorporate hard-coded Business Processes (BP), automatically executed without the awareness of their users. The models of these business processes serve a contemplative purpose, as a basis for specifying and modeling the software system. However, BPs evolve quickly, in the rhythm of the application domains, and their correspondences into program lines are difficult to understand and to change, so maintenance costs are high if work is performed at a low level of abstraction, that of the source code [4].

A well-known solution is to perform software maintenance at a higher level of abstraction [24]. Frequently, system architectures are designed such as to include explicit business processes, which are known to the various actors involved in configuration, maintenance, or even in the daily utilization of the system. These business process models can become productive if the architecture includes software artifacts for supporting their execution, with completely and /or partially automatic activities.

Let us take the example of Computer-Supported Cooperative Work (CSCW) domain, where classical tools include hard-coded coordination policies, but the adoption of explicitly defined, structured processes proved a significant increase of virtual teams' effectiveness [48]. The idea to provide automated support to process activities and agents was sustained by Process-centered Software Engineering Environments (PSEEs) [17]; e.g., by integrating SPADE for managing processes into the collaborative tool ImagineDesk [11], one provided process support to software developer organizations, particularly for conversation coordination and supervision. The awareness of the collaboration process has been proved to be very important in distributed teamwork, so it is necessary to define working models related to the way a group of individuals work together on a shared task [29].

The general aim is to empower various users with the possibility to choose among several processes, to adapt a process, to configure its execution and, moreover, to define new processes. The level of abstraction should be increased, and process modeling, including new designs and re-engineering, should be performed by domain experts exclusively. The open issue stands in the fact that, if one defines processes at a high level of abstraction, there is a need to transform them into an executable form. Moreover, if an enterprise decides to migrate to SOA (Service Oriented Architecture), the architecture should support the gradual replacement of manual activities by automatic ones (bound to services). Automation of business processes depends on the availability, for each process activity, of various services, located in different places and discovered at run-time. The activity/service mapping depends on predefined criteria, but also on the user preferences of the moment; service description may be performed using metadata [45]; markup languages [57] or domain ontologies [9] and may contain business information and quality characteristics.

Even if there is no classification of business processes that is generally accepted [27], it is obvious that they range from simple to very complex and this influences a lot the capabilities to automate them. For example, order fulfillment is generally simple, but it can be included in more complex processes related to purchasing and sales, which usually span across organizational borders. Inside an organization, the most complex process is considered to be the value chain, which can be composed of multiple core and support processes with the business goal of producing "a service, a product or a product line" [58]. Also, the process can be easier automated if the product that is obtained through it can be specified in advance and standardized, and if business rules exist [58]. The degree of automation of business processes is influenced by factors like:

- the existence of fully or partially automated activities, supported by software and organizational structures;
- the requirements for evolvability and adaptability, which may impose several levels of abstraction for the system architecture;
- the possibility to transform models from high abstraction levels into executable programs.

This chapter analyzes two existing approaches: the former based on large, general languages adopted as standards, and the latter based on small, but composable domain-specific languages. The following issues will be treated:

- *The spectrum of business process languages*
Subchapter 2 discusses the gap between modeling languages used by non-technical actors and programming languages, necessary for the execution of

service orchestration. Besides the adoption of many standards, the landscape of business process languages is still non-homogenous, and process languages need to be integrated with additional concerns, by extension, composition or transformation. Two types of languages are taken into account:

- general purpose languages, which attempt to be exhaustive and to grasp all possible situations;
- domain specific languages, which contain the core set of workflow concepts, but are conceived for being composed with other languages, for customizing the desired and the most appropriate high-level language.

- Software architectures for supporting business processes

Subchapter 3 outlines the role of Service Oriented Architectures, Semantic Web and Model Driven Engineering in creating systems for Business Process Management (BPM). Two solutions for modeling, executing and monitoring processes are presented: a multi-platform architecture based on adopted standards and a multi-domain architecture based on composing domain specific languages.

- Business process automation

Subchapter 4 investigates the vertical layers and the automation solutions for the two approaches, based on:

- successive transformations of models written in standard, general modeling languages, and
- direct interpretation of models expressed in a domain specific process language with its own interpreter as execution engine.

2. THE SPECTRUM OF BUSINESS PROCESS LANGUAGES

2.1. The Gap between Modeling and Execution

The landscape of business process modeling is fragmented and highly non-homogenous but, at the same time, there is a great effort for BPM standardization, based on 7 out of 10 formal groups dedicated to modeling [27]. Ko et al. propose a classification of BPM languages, standards and notations in four main groups: execution, interchange, graphical and diagnosis

[28]. We are interested here about two of them: graphical standards, corresponding to modeling at a high level of abstraction and accessible to business experts, and execution standards, which are essential for business process automation. Nowadays, the challenge is to fill in the gap between these two groups of languages, in order to pass seamlessly from modeling to automation. Actually, the dream is to obtain automation using friendly and intuitive graphical languages. Figure 18 presents a framework of business process languages, according to two kinds of actors: the Business Expert and the Technical Developer. Similarly, Lin et al. identify two types of actor-roles (social and technical actors) in a framework for semantic annotation of business processes [30]. This is also expressed by the business – IT duality identified in [63].

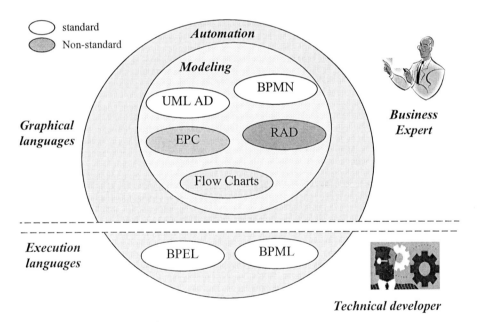

Figure 18. The landscape of business process languages.

For modeling business processes, there are two important graphical standards:

- *UML AD (UML Activity Diagrams)* – a language for workflows, included in the standard UML (Unified Modeling Language) adopted by Object Management Group (OMG) [39]; it is similar to flowcharts, but adding concurrency; moreover, there is also the UML Profile for Enterprise Distributed Object Computing (EDOC) [40] – an OMG standard for modeling business collaborations with UML, defining a community process on the top level; it pertains to the Model Driven Architecture (MDA) vision.

- *BPMN (Business Process Modeling Notation)* was adopted by OMG, under the Business Process Management Initiative (BPMI); it aims to supply a common notation for business analysts and technical developers, based on flowcharting [61] and it defines mappings for generating executable processes written in BPEL4WS (Business Process Execution Language for Web Services) [36].

Other examples of graphical languages, which are known and highly supported in academic and industrial environments, even if not standard, are: flow charts, Role-Activity Diagrams (RAD), Event-driven Process Chains (EPC). EPC is one of the most popular methods for modeling, analyzing, and redesigning business processes, based on directed graphs, with events and functions; it is supported by tools like ARIS, ADONIS, Business Process Visual ARCHITECT and Visio; as a standardization effort, one notices the definition of an XML-based interchange format for EPCs, called EPC Markup Language (EPML) [34].

On the other hand, there are other languages dedicated to the execution levels, which support the automation of business processes; this group contains two standards:

- *BPEL (Business Process Execution Language)* is a language based on XML (eXtensible Markup Language) standardized by OASIS [36]; it is the dominant standard encountered in software suites and has two versions:
    - BPEL4WS ver. 1.1 (Business Process Execution Language for Web Services) and
    - WS-BPEL ver. 2.0 (Web Service Business Process Execution Language) ver.2.0.

Furthermore, there are also BPEL4People [2] and WSHumanTask [3] - expected to eliminate some of the difficulties encountered at treating human tasks with WS-BPEL; this is important, as ethnographic analysis showed that it is not possible to completely eliminate work uncertainties and to have exclusively automated procedures [20]. Unfortunately, writing BPEL code is inaccessible to the business expert, as it is considerably more difficult than sequential programming [33].

- *BPML (Business Process Modeling Language)* is also based on XML (eXtensible Markup Language) and was adopted as standard by BPMI in 2002 [5]; despite the fact that it is considered a complete language, supporting both structure and semantics and incorporating human participation, it is no longer supported, after the merge of BPMI and OMG in 2005.

The possibilities for filling in this gap between the graphical languages used by non-technical actors, and the execution languages necessary for technical actors are discussed in subchapter 4.1, related to automation based on successive transformations of models.

2.2. Integrating Process Languages with Additional Concerns

The rapid evolution of businesses may involve changes of their processes, related to the succession of activities, the decision points, or the external events. In order to assure increased flexibility in process modeling, a problem is how one can separate various elements supposed to evolve from the basic workflow of the business process, for example to distinguish between process definitions and business rules [58]. Generally, these elements are hard-coded and implicitly introduced in process models.

Integrating process languages with additional concerns may be obtained by:

- extention - like enriching notations,
- composition with other kinds of models - for attaining executability or for automatic validation and
- transformation - to obtain models pertaining to another view.

Below, we present a series of integration approaches, ranging from particular to holistic ones, and summarized in Table 5.

- A) Rosenberg and Dustdar propose the integration of business rules in BPEL, based on SOA; BPEL is extended with a rule interceptor service, which automatically applies business rules to service calls [49].

B) zur Muehlen and Rosmann integrate business process models written in EPC with risk models [59].

C) In [51] a typical, graph-based process model, which can be mapped on existent languages like BPMN or Petri-nets, is annotated with flow, data, resource and time tags, representing control objectives and derived from FCL (Formal Contract Language) expressions.

D) Goedertier and Vanthienen define sequence and timing constraints expressed in PENELOPE language, verify for anomalies by analyzing the state-space, and then generate non-executable BPMN process models for validation [19].

E) In [31] the extension is performed with the purpose to check the compliance with legal requirements and international standards; BPEL process models are transformed into pi-calculus and then into Finite State Machines (FSM); on the other hand, compliance rules are modeled with BPSL (Business Property Specification Language) transformed into linear temporal logic and used for checking the models automatically; thus, one improves reliability by reducing the risk to deploy non-compliant business processes.

F) BREIN project creates a framework for a semantic integration of modeling languages [26]; in this context, one can generate a scenario ontology (written in OWL for example) out of multiple business process models expressed in E-BPMS; then one uses it for an assistant service that checks model consistency and makes suggestions to the business expert.

G) plugIT project chooses to externalize the expert knowledge by using graphical semi-formal models [63]; moreover, it introduces an IT-Socket model description framework, which opens the way to other extensions; process or workflow models can be mapped on models pertaining to 5 other aspects: Data/Knowledge, Process, Organization, Applications, Products and Motivation.

Table 5. Approaches for integrating process languages

Integration evaluation	Business Process Language	Additional Concern	Integration Method
A	BPEL	business rules	interceptor service
B	EPCs	risk models	extended notation
C	Graph-based process language	control objectives	annotations
D	BPMN	temporal deontic assignments	process model generation
E	BPEL	regulatory compliance	automated model checking
F	E-BPMS	scenario ontologies	assistance for checking model consistency
G	Languages of the Process aspect	models pertaining to 5 more aspects	ontology based transformations of models

Thus, business processes cover a wide range of topics and businesses, making virtually impossible to define a single high level language, in which all the BP aspects can be supported [14]. Despite the huge standardization efforts, there is still a landscape populated by incompatible languages and techniques, making complex and difficult to develop BP technology, and to write BP models.

2.3. A Domain Specific Process Language

As seen above, even languages meant to be general purpose require to be complemented with other formalisms. Therefore, research has been performed to find an alternative to the above state of practice. The basic idea is to replace the search for a high-level, generally efficient language, with a solution based on high-level, domain specific languages [62], complemented by a generic technology for their integration [22]. The composition of these DSLs allows building custom, high-level languages, fitting the needs of a specific business area; we call this the domain specific approach, where a domain is defined as an area in which a number of stakeholders are repeatedly performing similar activities.

A domain can be defined every time a set of engineering activities, practices, tools, methods or conventions shared by a group of persons is identified [54]. For a given software project, domains are defined by practitioners, given their experience and their desire to simplify, enforce, automate their common practices and separate them from other engineering activities. Domains are not necessarily independent in time and space, they can be active simultaneously, and can share some elements. An application pertaining to the domain can be defined by writing a model in its specific language, and its execution is based on the direct interpretation of this model, as described in subchapter 4.2.

In this approach, one of the most important pieces necessary for process-based applications is the Control Domain, based on the Abstract Process Engine Language APEL [13] for expressing the control model. APEL is a high level process language, containing a minimal set of concepts (presented in Figure 19), which are sufficient to express the purpose of a process model. An *activity* is a step of the process that involves the performance of an action, which is not defined into this process model, but can lean on invoking a service, running a program, or executing a human task. *Ports* represent the activity communication interface, each one specifying a list of expected products.

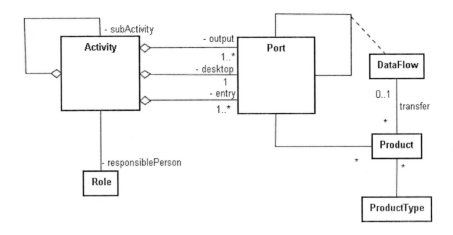

Figure 19. The APEL Language.

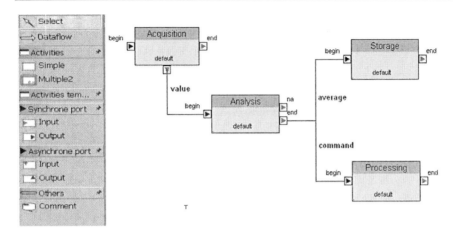

Figure 20. Alarm Control Model written in APEL.

A *product* is an object (i.e. record, data, file, document, etc) flowing between activities. Products are represented by variables that only have a type and a symbolic name (e.g. *"average"* is a product of type *"Computation"*). *Dataflows* connect output to input ports, specifying the product variables transferred from an activity to another.

Graphically, an activity is represented as a rectangle, ports are tiny squares situated on the activity border, a line connecting the ports denotes a dataflow, and labels on these dataflows represent products. This can be observed in Figure 20, presenting an APEL model of an alarm system: the *Acquisition* activity is in charge of collecting environment measures; the *Analysis* activity performs a computation over the gathered data; finally, two parallel activities are executed: the former - *Storage* - makes the data persistent, and the latter - *Processing* - triggers an action in case of abnormal data values.

3. SOFTWARE ARCHITECTURES FOR SUPPORTING BUSINESS PROCESSES

Software support for business processes is influenced by the convergence of three important research domains:

- Service Oriented Architectures

In an environment of continuously evolving businesses, there is a strong demand for a fast adaptation to new requirements and for assimilating new business processes and service providers. Service Oriented Architecture [55] offers solutions for nowadays problems, by supporting atomic and composite services, eventually delivered by multiple cross-border service providers. SOA supports widely distributed software artifacts and increases flexibility and extensibility with late-bound services, discovered at runtime [10]. There are more and more business processes based on cross enterprise cooperation, due to outsourcing or enterprise merging. With the newly demands for increasing the scale, large frameworks and infrastructures are developed, supporting billions of parties that expose and consume Web services (SOA4All) [53] or creating clouds (RESERVOIR) [47].

- Semantic Web

More technical and conceptual problems are generated by the necessity to create large-scale distributed systems, based on one-stop portals for accessing a large variety of processes, characteristic to multiple organizations. In these situations, semantic non-homogeneity can be treated by defining ontologies [18] for characterizing generic processes, abstract Web services, service providers and quality of service (QoS) metrics. For avoiding predefined mappings between abstract and concrete services and for taking into account quality criteria and user choices, SOA is grounded on semantic Web services. Moreover, the use of reference ontologies mapped on local ones has become a solution for the interoperability between heterogeneous systems [9], as well as for managing the system content and its changes [56].

- Model Driven Engineering

With Model Driven Engineering (MDE) [16] one can obtain descriptive or executable specifications at a high level of abstraction, creating libraries of models and metamodels, which can be easily integrated, reused and adapted. This approach has encouraged working with explicitly defined process models, elaborated by business domain experts, using friendly editors; moreover, processes can become executable by orchestrating web services, components or tools.

Two examples of architectures based on process management are given below: a multi-platform architecture taking advantage of the general, standard languages for modeling and executing processes (see 4.1) and a multi-domain architecture based on composing domain specific languages (see 4.2).

3.1. Multi-platform Architecture for Modeling and Executing Processes

This subchapter presents a SOA architecture for modeling, executing and monitoring a system built for the seamless integration of heterogeneous types of cross-border business services. The challenge is to eliminate the loose electronic integration of activities for Service Providers (SPs) from various countries and regions, as well as to improve service/process reconfiguration and maintenance and to propagate semantic definition changes to registered services and processes. This architecture was adopted for LD-CAST project (Local Development Cooperation Actions Enabled by Semantic Technology) [32]. The vertical dimension of this architecture and the way services are orchestrated are described in subchapter 4.1.

3.1.1. Process Management Subsystems

The SOA architecture is composed of three platforms, related through web services, dedicated for modeling, execution and administration of business services supplied by various regional and /or national chambers of commerce [6]. We analyze below the four subsystems related to process management (see Figure 21):

- *Business Process Modeler (BP Modeler)* – pertaining to the *Modeling Platform* – is used by the Business Process Designer for modeling business processes with ADOeGov modeling language [41], annotating their activities with concepts from the domain ontology and storing them; there are specific components for: editing models, searching the repository, importing/exporting and introducing semantic annotations;

- *Run Time Portal* – pertaining to the *Execution Platform* - is used by the End-User for obtaining information and business services, delivered by interaction with other subsystems. It is implemented with JEM (JBoss Enterprise Middleware) [25] and also supports the involvement of the correspondent actors in certain activities that contain human tasks, by offering a console to monitor business service requests and check their progress and status. Moreover, the End-User can interact with the system during the workflow execution for filling-in forms, uploading documents, downloading results, or starting manual activities. The choice was to embed human tasks inside generic, core web services, which sometimes contain processes that orchestrate other services in their turn.

- *Process Execution Management (PEM)* - pertaining to the *Execution Platform* - is in charge of executing the processes corresponding to the business service selected by users; it stores the process instance state, which can be monitored from the Run-Time Portal. PEM transforms abstract workflows into concrete ones, taking into account the user preferences for determining the set of concrete web services; it uses ActiveBPEL engine for executing workflows written in BPEL4WS;

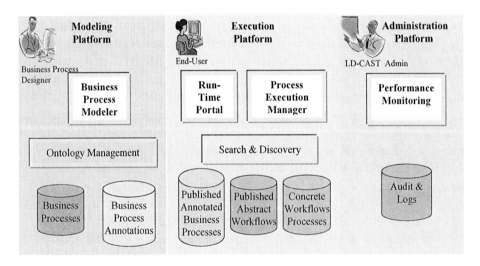

Figure 21. Process management in a multi-platform architecture.

- *Performance Monitoring* – pertaining to the *Administration Platform* - collects logs from subsystems of Modeling and Execution Platforms, such as to offer a centralized monitoring console to the LD-CAST Administrator. For each process model, it displays graphical and numerical representations for criteria like: number of requests, execution times, or number of concrete service configurations.

Furthermore, there are other subsystems with an important impact on process management, which are related to the way processes are defined and executed:

-   *Ontology Manager* – pertaining to the *Modeling Platform* – serves for defining and maintaining the business domain ontology, used for characterizing both modeling elements (processes, activities) and implementation ones (web services). One uses OPAL (Object, Process, Actor Modeling Language) [8]. Thus, the concepts familiar to the domain expert and the relationships between them are also useful at run time, by defining criteria for performing various transformations and matches between abstract and concrete services;
-   *Search & Discovery* – pertaining to the *Execution Platform* – searches and discovers the most appropriate atomic Web services that are registered at LD-CAST and satisfy the needs of the End User; these concrete services are bound to the process models at run-time, such as to be able to execute them.

3.1.2. Subsystems Involved in a Typical Scenario

A typical scenario performed by the End-User is related to the management of business services - complex, composite services, which can be realized by various processes that orchestrate web services. The activity diagram for such a scenario is represented in Figure 22.

The first step is to select the business service, for which the Portal displays the available services and their descriptions, obtained from the Business Process Modeler, where they correspond to groups of processes.

After that, one selects the preferred business process, on the basis of description made in structured natural language, also available from BP Modeler. Actually, the user is not aware of the process model from the backstage; he or she chooses Company Legal Verification for example, realized in Italy, for releasing a document specifically called "Visura". This activity involves more complex interactions in the backstage, for allowing flexibility and taking into account user preferences.

Then, the Portal has to search for configurations of concrete Web services that can be used for the actual execution. This step involves more complex interactions in the backstage, to permit flexibility and take into account user preferences. For the previously selected business process, there is a correspondent abstract workflow in PEM repositories. It represents the sequencing of operations in the control flow, but activities do not have concrete implementations. For creating a concrete workflow, mappings on concrete services are necessary. A set of registered Web services, matching to inputs, outputs and semantics of the abstract activities is called configuration. This semantic matchmaking is done by the Search & Discovery subsystem, which interacts with the Run-Time Portal. For a certain business process, there can be more such configurations suitable for being executed. The End-User selects one of them, in respect with the expected execution time, its cost, service provider and other information related to the quality of service, and then starts the execution of that business process.

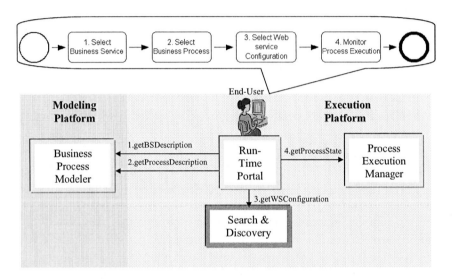

Figure 22. Subsystems involved for Business Service Management.

Finally, one monitors the process execution, when the Portal gets information related to the process state from the Process Execution Manager. The End-User checks the progress and status of the requested business service with a console of the Run-Time Portal.

3.2. Multi-domain Architecture for Business Processes

This subchapter presents a multi-domain architecture, which allows the separation of various concerns related to business processes into different domains, which are driven by DSLs and are composable at a high level of abstraction. An essential part is the Control domain, whose domain specific language is APEL, described in subchapter 2.3. The vertical dimension of this architecture, including the mechanisms for mapping activities on executable artifacts (services and others) is described in subchapter 4.2.

3.2.1. The Business Process Composite Domain

A domain is conceived as a unit of reuse that is autonomous and composable at the meta-level of abstraction, that of its domain specific language; thus, one eliminates dependencies on the implementation techniques and details. Moreover, these domains are configurable through models defined in their specific languages, and applications pertaining to these domains are driven by the interpretation of their correspondent models. The domain composition approach allows the definition of a core Business Process domain, from which various BPM tools can be built. An operational business process system is therefore the core Business Process domain, customized to fit the actual needs, or composed with other specific domains to cover further aspects. Thus, one can reuse existent domains developed in time, according to customer needs, like: product, security, dynamic services, workspace management, versioning, software development and so on.

As seen in Figure 23, the core Business Process domain can be composed with other domains, and it is itself the composition of the following sub-domains [44]:

- **Control** domain - expressing the execution ordering;
- **Service** domain - defining the computations to be performed;
- **Data** domain - defining the information on which the execution is to be performed, and
- **Resources** domain - defining how humans are involved in performing the business process.

The mechanism for composing Control with other domains, in order to create a composite domain, is presented in subchapter 3.2.2. The advantage brought by this separation is the possibility to express the workflow logic in the control model, irrespective of collateral details related to the underlying services, and independent from organizational structures or data, which can rely, for example, on existent user management systems (generally available for the project managers in each company) and on information systems in place.

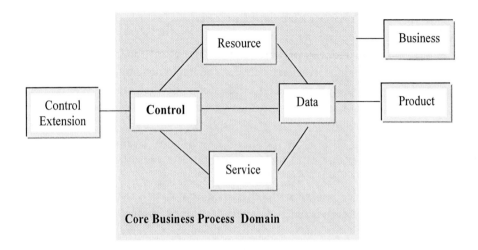

Figure 23. Business Process composite domain.

3.2.2. Composition of Control Domain

A domain is characterized by a DSL covering a narrow and strongly coupled range of concepts, so it has to be composed for developing large-scale applications. Composing two domains requires specifying correspondences at two levels of abstraction: i) relationships between concepts of their DSLs, called metalinks, and ii) relationships between elements of the models conforming to them, called links. If a metalink is defined between two concepts pertaining to APEL and DSL_X for example (see Figure 24), then links must be defined between some instances conforming to them, i.e. links must be defined between elements of APEL_Model and Model_X.

Figure 25 exemplifies how the generic model composition can be applied to compose Control and Data models. It is based on a metalink defined between the *ProductType* concept in APEL, and the *DataType* concept in Data DSL. In APEL, a *ProductType* has a symbolic name only, grasping nothing related to the nature of products flowing between activities. On the other side, in Data DSL, the structure of entities is defined without knowing anything about the actions performed on them. In this example, the metalink allows the specification of what is really transmitted from an activity to another.

Domain (Control + X)

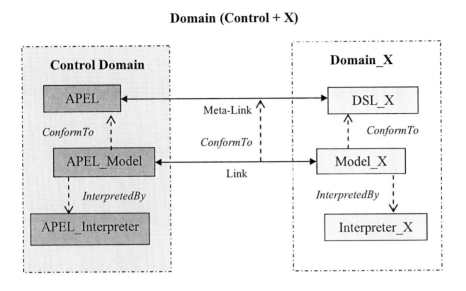

Figure 24. Domain Composition Schema.

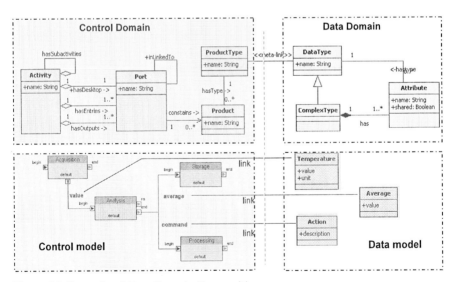

Figure 25. Control and Data Domain Composition.

In the lower part of Figure 25, model composition for an alarm system is presented. At model level, there are links between instances of the two concepts related by a meta-link. The composition defines that a *value* (in

Control model) corresponds to a *Temperature* (in Data model); similarly, there are links between *average* and *Average*, *command* and *Action*. Model composition is realized without modification of the original models, thus significantly increasing the reuse possibilities. The same Control model can also be composed with another Data model, so *value* can be mapped on *Pressure* for example, instead of *Temperature*.

In order to provide the capability to execute the composed models, domain interpreters also have to be composed, based on the meta-link definitions; all the public methods of the concepts involved in a relationship are intercepted, such as, at their invocation, to be able to perform the appropriate actions in the related domain. Additional code must be written to define the composition semantics. In the particular case of *Control* and *Data* domains, when a *Product* is created in the control interpreter, a corresponding *Data* is created in the data interpreter.

4. BUSINESS PROCESS AUTOMATION

In order to pass from high level modeling to concrete execution, so to obtain the automation of business processes, the layered conception of BPM systems, in a form or another, is generally admitted. Karagiannis et al. define three layers: for business models, workflow models and execution models [26]. Papazoglou proposes six levels of abstraction: domains layer, business processes, business services, infrastructure services, service realizations, operational systems [42]. A layered approach is also introduced in [28], by identifying graphical, interchange and execution standards.

Two solutions of automation are discussed below:

- the use of a general modeling language for defining business processes, like BPMN, and then the transformation into executable BPEL workflows, for which execution engines already exist (see subchapter 4.1) and
- the use of a Domain Specific Language for defining process models and of the DSL interpreter as execution engine (see subchapter 4.2) .

4.1. Automation Based on Successive Transformations of Models

Besides the integration of various concerns, the system architecture has to assure the mappings between business activities from the high level process models defined by domain experts and the existent web services. This subchapter presents the solution based on transformation of models expressed with general modeling languages, where one identifies five layers of abstraction (see
Figure 26) [21]:

- the *Modeling Layer* – standing in business processes modeled by experts in the application domain, using BPMN or other editors;
- the *Execution Layers* – consisting in BPEL workflows written by a programmer:
    - *Abstract Execution* – orchestrating abstract activities;
    - *Concrete Execution* – orchestrating activities bound at the implementation artifacts;
- the *Service Layers* - made of Web services that can be invoked in BPEL for the execution of the process:
    - *Abstract Services* - a class of similar services, defined by the same functionality, input, output and, eventually, by other non-functional properties;
    - *Concrete Services* – available implementations of services, which can be invoked and orchestrated.

Writing executable workflows in BPEL is too complicated for the business experts, so business processes are defined at a high level of abstraction, but they have to be transformed into executable BPEL code, in order to assure the system automation. Transformation criteria are given in the standard specification of BPMN [38], but generation of BPEL code encounters important limitations. An analysis of the context for generating workflows from process models can be found in [50]; different process engines require different workflow code, and domain-specific models need complex graph transformation algorithms, for coming from a graph-based to a block-based structure.

A bi-directional BPMN – BPEL mapping would fill the gap between business and technical actors, as well as between design and implementation of processes. Currently, translations from graphical languages from the Modeling Layer, like BPMN, to execution languages like BPEL is partially supported and it is included in many BPM systems. One generally admits that it is more difficult the other way around [28]; Weidlich et al. analyzed the mismatches for BPEL to BPMN translation and proposed to introduce supplementary constructs in BPMN (in respect to its 1.1. version) [60]. Despite this, the study of Recker and Mendling [46] proves that, in turn, the complex concepts from BPMN cannot be entirely translated into executable BPEL and should be restricted. They discuss the conceptual mismatches between BPMN and BPEL regarding the representation capability, control flow, and process representation paradigm. Generally, for the Modeling Layer, there are graphical languages, with diagrams oriented on graphs; for the Execution Layers, there are languages that represent control flow by nesting blocks; they have difficulties to render cyclical and temporal elements from the diagrams; in turn, their support for recurrence cannot be supported through graphics [28]; therefore, transformations between them are subject to information loss.

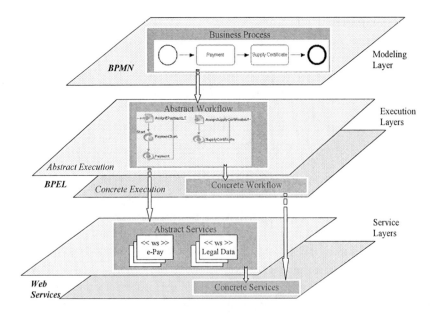

Figure 26. Automation Layers with General Modeling Languages.

Instead of using a direct mapping, another possibility to translate graphic to execution standards is to use interchange standards:

- XPDL (XML Process Definition Language) was adopted by WfMC [64] and was considered ideal for translating from BPMN to BPEL and other execution standards based on XML;
- BPDM (Business Process Definition Metamodel) was adopted by OMG [37]; it is based on XML and includes abstractions of the common elements of various business process modeling languages, like UML AD, BPMN, BPEL.

Despite the dream of complete automation and transformations, there are still stages that cannot be completely automated. In order to offer support for collaboration of different stakeholders and integrate business and IT perspectives, plugIT project proposes a holistic Next Generation Modeling Framework (NGMF), including vertical and horizontal transformations of models written in various languages, based on semantic technology [63].

4.2. Automation Based on Direct Interpretation of Models

In the approach based on composition of domains driven by specific languages, the automation of business processes depends on two key issues:

- the composition of the central Control sub-domain with the other sub-domains, like Data, Service and Resource and
- the executability of the Control process models defined in APEL by the domain experts.

For the first key issue, the domain composition leans on DSL composition [15], performed at design time, and model composition, which can be performed either at design time, or automatically, at run-time [22]. At the implementation of a DSL interpreter, one has to respect specific conventions for mapping the language concepts to the target programming language, because the result has to be composable with other domain interpreters. The target implementation language must be able to express the DSL operational semantics, so it is convenient to use an object-oriented programming language, like Java or C++, or an executable metamodeling language, like Kermeta [35] or XMF (eXecutable Metamodelling Facility) [7]; executable metamodeling languages allow not only the description of the model structure (the abstract syntax), but also of the behavior.

Regarding the second key issue, models can be executable only if the semantic part of the DSL is rich enough to fully describe the model behavior. For modeling a workflow, the APEL editor uses the abstract syntax (AS) of the language, containing concepts and rules necessary to define a valid model. Most modern meta-tools (e.g. Eclipse Modeling Framework) rely on AS for generating editors. However, for building an interpreter one needs a strong Semantic Domain (SD) for providing the meaning of the abstract syntax concepts. Following most meta-environment strategy, at execution time, the model is transformed (reified) into instances of the abstract syntax classes.

The translation from modeling with APEL to executing these models passes through the following layers (see Figure 27) [43]:

- the *Logical Layers* – for designing the business logic and the orchestration annotations:
    - the *Modeling Layer* – consisting in workflows written by a business expert, using the APEL specific language;
    - the *Orchestration / Choreography Layer* – optionally used for specifying a distributed orchestration, combined with choreography, at a high level of abstraction;
- the *Binding Layer* – for discovery and invocation of services, using a Service Abstract Machine (SAM) and mediators for solving syntactic incompatibilities;
- the *Physical Layer* – characterized by non-homogeneity and populated by services implemented in various technologies: Web services, OSGi, EJB and Java.

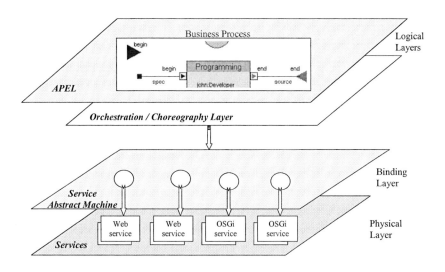

Figure 27. Automation Layers with Domain Specific Languages.

CONCLUSION

The current requirements for rapid evolution cycles demand solutions that avoid the existing gap between business experts and technical developers, from the point of view of theoretical background, experience, dedicated languages, and tools. Despite the fact that their contributions are both of major importance for developing the system, one has generated problems related to transformation between different formalisms accepted by both sides, and to difficulties of understanding each other's points of view. A sensible solution would be to diminish the high coupling of their activities, at least in the maintenance stage. In this context, the transition from contemplative towards imperative roles of business process models is considered essential. Thus, business experts could actually act on the system, by updating models, business rules, or domain ontology concepts.

Ideally, a high level and general business process formalism would be both technology independent and dedicated to business experts; however, it is very difficult in practice to be abstract, generic and efficient at the same time. Classical approaches are generally based on a dichotomy, where standard, but different languages are used for modeling and execution of business processes. Consequently, general purpose, high level languages, like BPMN, require vertical mappings and transformations into various execution oriented languages, like BPEL. Currently, this translation cannot be performed entirely automatically, and, moreover, the obstacles stand in the natures of languages themselves. Alternatively, approaches based on domain specific languages have the advantage of model executability, which empowers the domain experts and assures a smooth evolution of the system. However, DSLs are generally conceived for a high degree of reusability, so their scope is usually narrow, and they have to be further composed for creating large-scale applications.

REFERENCES

[1] P.S. Adler, A. Mandelbaum, V. Nguyen and E. Schwerer, From Project to Process Management: An Empirically-Based Framework for Analyzing Product Development Time, *Management Science*, Vol. 41, No. 3, 1995, pp. 458-484

[2] Agrawal, M. Amend, M. Das, M. Ford, M., C. Keller, M. Kloppmann, D. König, F. Leymann, R. Müller, G. Pfau, K. Plösser, R. Rangaswamy, A. Rickayzen, M. Rowley, P. Schmidt, I. Trickovic, A. Yiu, and M. Zeller, *WS-BPEL Extension for People (BPEL4People)*, version 1.0, 2007

[3] Agrawal, M. Amend, M. Das, M. Ford, M., C. Keller, M. Kloppmann, D. König, F. Leymann, R. Müller, G. Pfau, K. Plösser, R. Rangaswamy, A. Rickayzen, M. Rowley, P. Schmidt, I. Trickovic, A. Yiu, and M. Zeller, *Web Services Human Task (WSHumanTask)*, version 1.0, 2007.

[4] K. H. Bennett, V.T. Rajlich, Software Maintenance and Evolution: a Roadmap, from *The Future of Software Engineering*, Anthony Finkelstein (Ed.), ACM Press, 2000

[5] BPMI, Business Process Management Initiative , Available: http://www.bpmi.org/ Accessed: August 8, 2010

[6] Catapano, A. D'Atri, V. Hrgovcic, A.D. Ionita, and K. Tarabanis, LD-CAST: Local Development Cooperation Actions Enabled by Semantic Technology, In *Proceedings of Eastern European eGov Days Conference, EEGOV,* Prague, Czech Republic, April 23-25, 2008

[7] T. Clark and al., *Applied metamodelling – a foundation for language driven development version 0.1.* Xactium, Editor, 2004.

[8] F. D'Antonio, M. Missikoff and F. Taglino, Formalizing the OPAL eBusiness ontology design patterns with OWL, *Proc.of the Third International Conference on Interoperability for Enterprise Applications and Software, I-ESA 2007*, Funchal, Portugal, March 28-30, 2007

[9] E. Della Valle, D. Cerizza, I. Celino, J. Estublier, G. Vega, M. Kerrigan, J. Ram'ırez, B. Villazon, P. Guarrera, G. Zhao, and G. Monteleone, SEEMP: an Semantic Interoperability Infrastructure for e-government services in the employment sector, *Lecture Notes in Computer Science*, 5419, 2007, pp. 220-234

[10] DG Information Society and Media - Directorate for Converged Networks and Services, Future Internet Assemble 2009, *Conference Report, Stockholm, Sweden*, 23rd– 24th November 2009

[11] E. Di Nitto, A. Fuggetta, Integrating Process Technology and CSCW, Lecture Notes in Computer Science, Vol. 913, 1995, pp. 154-161

[12] D.S. Eppinger, Generalized models of design interaction using signal flow graphs, *Research in Engineering Design*, Vol. 9, 1997, pp. 112-123

[13] J. Estublier, S. Dami, M. Amiour, Apel: A graphical yet executable formalism for process modeling, *Automated Software Engineering: An International Journal*, Vol. 5, No. 1, 1998, pp. 61–96

[14] J. Estublier and S. Sanlaville, Extensible Process Support Environments for Web Services Orchestration. *International Journal of Web Services Practices* (IJWSP), Vol. 1, No. 1-2, 2005, pp. 30-39

[15] J. Estublier, G. Vega, A.D. Ionita, Composing Domain-Specific Languages for Wide-Scope Software Engineering Applications, *Lecture Notes in Computer Science, Proceeding of MoDELS/UML Conference*, Jamaica, 3713, 2005, pp. 69 – 83

[16] J.M. Favre, Towards a Basic Theory to Model Driven Engineering, *3rd Workshop in Software Model Engineering, WiSME* 2004

[17] V. Gruhn, Process-Centered Software Engineering Environments, A Brief History and Future Challenges, *Annals of Software Engineering*, Vol. 14, No. 1-4, 2002, pp. 363-382

[18] D. Gašević, D. Djurić, V.Devedžić, *Model Driven Architecture and Ontology Development*, Springer-Verlag, 2006

[19] S. Goedertier J. Vanthienen, Designing Compliant Business Processes with Obligations and Permissions, J. Eder, S. Dustdar et al. (Eds.) *BPM 2006 Workshops, LNCS,* 4103, Springer Verlag, 2006

[20] N. Hayes, Work-arounds and Boundary Crossing in a High Tech Optronics Company: The Role of Co-operative Workflow Technologies, *Computer Supported Cooperative Work*, 9, 2000, pp. 435-455

[21] A.D. Ionita, A. Catapano, S. Giuroiu, and M. Florea, Service oriented system for business cooperation, Proceedings of *Int. Workshop on Systems Development in SOA Environments ICSE/SDSOA '08*, Leipzig, Germany, May 11, ACM, New York, 2008, pp. 13-18.

[22] A.D. Ionita, J. Estublier, Th. Leveque, T. Nguyen, Bi-dimensional Composition with Domain Specific Languages, *e-Informatica Software Engineering Journal*, Vol. 3, No. 1, 2009, pp. 27-41

[23] A.D. Ionita, M. Florea, L. Jelea, 4+1 Views for a Business Cooperation Framework Based on SOA, *IAENG International Journal of Computer Science*, Vol. 36, No. 4, 2009, pp. 332-343

[24] A.D. Ionita, M. Litoiu, Evolvability In Service Oriented Systems, *Proceedings of the Fifth International Conference on Software and Data Technologies, INSTICC / ICSOFT 2010*, Athens, Greece, July 22 - 24, 2010, pp. 245-250

[25] JBoss Enterprise Middleware, Available: http://www.jboss.com, Accessed: August, 8, 2010

[26] D. Karagiannis, W. Utz, R. Woitsch, H. Eichner, BPM4SOA Business Process Models for Semantic Service-Oriented Infrastructures, in P. Cunningham and M. Cunningham (Eds), *Collaboration and the Knowledge Economy: Issues, Applications, Case Studies*, IOS Press, 2008

[27] R.K.L. Ko, A Computer Scientist's Introductory Guide to Business Process Management, *Crossroads*, Vol. 15, No.4, 2009

[28] R. K. L. Ko, S. S. G. Lee, and E. W. Lee, Business process management (BPM) standards: A survey, *Business Process Management Journal,* Vol. 15, No. 5, 2009

[29] P. Leinonen, S. Järvelä, P. Häkkinen, Conceptualizing the Awareness of Collaboration: A Qualitative Study of a Global Virtual Team, *Computer Supported Cooperative Work*, Vol. 14, Springer, 2005, pp. 301-322

[30] Y. Lin, J. Krogstie, Quality Evaluation of a Business Process Semantic Annotations Approach, *IBIS*, Vol. 3, No. 1, 2009, pp. 9-29

[31] Y. Liu, S. Müller, K. Xu, A static compliance-checking framework for business process models, *IBM Systems Journal*, Vol. 46, No. 2, 2007

[32] LD-CAST project (Local Development Coordination Actions enabled by Semantic Technology) Available: http://www.ldcastproject.com Accessed: August, 9, 2010

[33] Ma, Q. Xu and J.W. Sanders, *A Survey of Business Process Execution Language (BPEL)*, UNU-IIST Report No. 425, 2009

[34] J. Mendling, M. Nüttgens, *EPC Markup Language (EPML) - An XML-Based Interchange Format for Event-DrivenProcess Chains (EPC)*, Technical Report JM-2005-03-10, Vienna University of Economics and Business Administration, 2005

[35] P.A. Muller, F. Fleurey, and J.M. Jézéquel, Weaving executability into object-oriented meta-languages, *Lecture Notes in Computer Science, Proceedings of the MoDELS/UML* Conference, Jamaica, 2005

[36] OASIS, Web Services Business Process Execution Language for Web Services, Version 2.0, 2007. Available: http://docs.oasis-open.org/wsbpel/2.0/wsbpel-v2.0.pdf   Accessed: August 8, 2010

[37] OMG, *Business Process Definition Metamodel (BPDM)*, Version 1.0, Available at: http://www.omg.org/spec/BPDM, Accessed: August 8, 2010

[38] OMG, *Business Process Modeling Notation (BPMN)*, Version 1.2, OMG Document Number: formal/2009-01-03, Available at: http://www.omg.org/spec/BPMN/1.2, Accessed: August 8, 2010

[39] OMG, *UML 2.0 Superstructure Specification*, 2005. Available: http://www.omg.org/technology/documents/formal/uml.htm, Accessed : August 8, 2010

[40] OMG, UML Profile for enterprise distributed Object Computing (EDOC), http://www.omg.org/technology/documents/formal/edoc.htm Accessed: August 8, 2010

[41] S. Palkovits, D. Orensanz, D. Karagiannis, Process modelling in Egovernment – Living process modelling within a public organisation, *IADIS International Conferece e-Society*, 2004, pp. 3-10.

[42] M. P. Papazoglou, *Web services: Principles and technology*, Prentice-Hall, 2007

[43] G. Pedraza and J. Estublier, Distributed Orchestration versus Choreography: The FOCAS Approach, *Lecture Notes in Computer Science*, Vol. 5543, 2009, pp. 75-86

[44] G. Pedraza, I. Dieng, , J. Estublier, Multi-concerns composition for a process support framework, Berlin, *Proceedings of the Workshop on Model Driven Tool and Process Integration, ECMDA,* June 9, 2008

[45] V. Peristeras, and K. Tarabanis, Reengineering the public administration modus operandi through the use of reference domain models and Semantic Web Service technologies, *Proc. of the AAAI Spring Symposium on The Semantic Web meets eGovernment (SWEG)* Stanford University, California, USA Mar. 27-29, 2006

[46] J. Recker and J. Mendling, On the Translation between BPMN and BPEL: Conceptual Mismatch between Process Modeling Languages, *Proceedings of the Workshop on Exploring Modeling Methods for Systems Analysis and Design (EMMSAD'06)*, Luxemburg, 2006, pp. 521-532

[47] RESERVOIR project, Available: http://www.reservoir-fp7.eu/ Accessed: August, 9, 2010

[48] D.J. Rice, B.D. Davidson, J.F. Dannenhoffer, G.K. Gay, Improving the Effectiveness of Virtual Teams by Adapting Team Processes, *Computer Supported Cooperative Work,* Vol. 16, Springer 2007, pp.567-594

[49] F. Rosenberg, S. Dustdar, Business Rules Integration in BPEL – A Service-Oriented Approach, *Proc. Of the 7th Int. Conf. on Service Oriented Computing, CEC'05*, 2005,pp. 476-479

[50] St. Roser, F. Lautenbacher, and B. Bauer, Generation of workflow code from DSMs, *Proceedings of the 7th OOPSLA Workshop on Domain-Specific Modeling*, Montreal, Canada, October 2007

[51] S. Sadiq, G. Governatori, K. Namiri, Modeling Control Objectives for Business Process Compliance, *5th Int. Conference on Business Process Management*, Brisbane, Australia, 2007

[52] W. Scacchi , Process Models in Software Engineering, in J.J. Marciniak (ed.), *Encyclopedia of Software Engineering*, 2nd Edition, John Wiley and Sons, Inc., New York, December 2001

[53] SOA4ALL) Project (Service Oriented Architectures for All), Available: http://www.soa4all.eu Accessed: August, 10, 2010

[54] M. Simos, Organization Domain Modeling and OO Analysis and Design: Distinctions, Integration, New Directions, *STJA'97 Conf. Proc.*, Technische Universität Ilemenau, Thüringen, 1997, pp. 126-132

[55] J. Sommerville, *Software Engineering*, 8th Edition, Addison-Wesley, 2006

[56] N. Stojanovic, G. Mentzas, D. Apostolou, Semantic-enabled Agile Knowledge-based e-government, *AAAI Spring Symposium "The Semantic Web meets eGovernment"*, Stanford University, California, USA, March 27-29, 2006

[57] E. Tambouris, An Integrated Platform for Realizing One-Stop Government: The eGOV project, *E-Government Workshop within DEXA01*, IEEE Press, pp. 359-363

[58] W.J. van den Heuvel (Ed.), *Survey on Business Process Management*, S-CUBE Deliverable # PO-JRA-2.1.1, 2008

[59] M. zur Muehlen, M. Rosmann, Integrating Risks in Business Process Models, *16th Australasian Conf. on Information Systems*, Sydney, Australia, 2005

[60] M. Weidlich, G. Decker, A. Großkopf, and M. Weske, BPEL to BPMN: The Myth of a Straight-Forward Mapping, Lecture Notes in Computer Science, Vol. 5331, 2008, pp. 265-282

[61] St. A. White, Introduction to BPMN, BPTrends, July, 2004, Available: ww.bptrends.com Accessed: August, 9, 2010

[62] A.S. Wile., Supporting the DSL Spectrum, *Journal of Computing and Information Technology*, CIT, Vol. 9, No. 4, 2001, pp. 263-287

[63] R. Woitsch, D. Karagiannis, D. Plexousakis, K. Hinkelmann, Business and IT alignment: the IT-Socket, *Elektrotechnik & Informationstechnik,* Springer-Verlag, 126/7/8, 2009, pp. 308–321.

[64] XPDL XML Process Definition Language, Available at: http://www.wfmc.org/xpdl.html, Accessed 7 Aug. 2010

In: Business Process Modeling
Editor: Jason A. Beckmann

ISBN: 978-1-61209-344-4
©2011 Nova Science Publishers, Inc.

Chapter 4

TOWARDS CONCISE ARCHITECTURES FOR FLEXIBLE BUSINESS PROCESSES

Udo Kannengiesser and Liming Zhu[*]

NICTA, Australia, and School of Computer Science and Engineering,
University of New South Wales, Sydney, Australia

ABSTRACT

This chapter proposes a view of business processes as designed artefacts that are ontologically no different than artefacts in domains such as mechanical and software engineering. This view distinguishes three concerns for designing processes: architecture, implementation and adaptation. We show that current process modelling approaches conflate these aspects, often leading to high complexity and inflexibility of the resulting process models. We use a generalisation of the "feature" concept in engineering design, represented using the function-behaviour-structure (FBS) ontology, as the basis of a new approach to concisely specifying business process architectures that allow for more process flexibility.

---

[*] {udo.kannengiesser, liming.zhu}@nicta.com.au

1. INTRODUCTION

Business process modelling is an area that deals with creating representations of business processes for various purposes, including business process analysis, understanding, communication, standardisation, simulation, improvement and implementation. Although a number of different, mostly graphical notations and tools for modelling business processes have been developed (Dumas et al. 2005), their effectiveness is often reduced due to a number of issues that remain topics of ongoing research. One of the issues is the high complexity of many process models, which significantly affects understanding of these models by human experts (Bandara et al. 2007). This problem is commonly perceived as a problem of model granularity, to be addressed by striking a balance between comprehensibility and level of detail.

Another issue is the poor flexibility of most business process models (Regev et al. 2007). Factors such as market or strategy changes, technological innovations and new regulations often require modifications of a process. Furthermore, unforeseen events in the immediate environment of the process may need to be handled flexibly, such as resource bottlenecks or effects of unexpected human or system errors. Process models that are too rigidly defined are poorly applicable in real-world contexts and are ultimately rejected by their users.

In this chapter, we argue that the issues of complexity and flexibility of process models are due to an inadequate understanding of processes as designed artefacts. Drawing analogies with the domains of mechanical and software engineering, we develop a framework that clarifies the distinction between three concerns in process design (Kannengiesser 2009a): architecture, implementation and adaptation. We show that current business process modelling approaches conflate these aspects, often leading to high complexity and inflexibility of the resulting process models. We use a generalisation of the "feature" concept in engineering design, represented using the function-behaviour-structure (FBS) ontology (Gero 1990; Gero and Kannengiesser 2004), as the basis of a new approach to concisely specifying process architectures that allow for more process flexibility. We demonstrate our approach using examples of a property valuation process in the mortgage industry.

2. ARTEFACTS

Artefacts can be defined as entities made by humans to achieve a set of objectives. They can be modelled using the function-behaviour-structure (FBS) ontology (Gero 1990; Gero and Kannengiesser 2004) that has been applied to various instances of artefacts, including physical products (Gero and Kannengiesser 2004), software (Kruchten 2005) and processes (Gero and Kannengiesser 2007).

Structure (S) is defined as an artefact's components and their relationships ("what the artefact consists of"). It can be viewed as the final outcome of a design process. In the domain of physical products, structure comprises the geometry, topology and material of individual components or assemblies (Gero 1990). The structure of software consists of more abstract concepts that cannot be perceived directly using human sensory capabilities. It "exists" only as a set of high-level constructs, represented graphically or symbolically. In the domain of processes, structure includes three classes of interrelated components: input, transformation and output (Gero and Kannengiesser 2007). Here, the transformation often consists of a coherent set of sub-transformations (or sub-processes). Similar to software structure, most of the individual components of process structure are fairly abstract entities that are often described using boxes and arrows.

Behaviour (B) is defined as the attributes that can be derived from an artefact's structure ("what the artefact does"). An example of a physical product's behaviour is "weight", which can be derived (or measured) from the product's structure properties of material and spatial dimensions. Behaviour of software (e.g., a text editor) includes its response time for visualising user input. It can be derived from software structure and its interaction with the (e.g., operating) environment. Typical behaviours of processes include speed, cost, precision and accuracy. They can also be derived from structure properties; for example, speed can be derived from time stamps on input and output.

Function (F) is defined as an artefact's teleology ("what the artefact is for"). This notion is independent of the common distinction between "functional" and "non-functional" properties; it comprises both as long as long as they describe the artefact's usefulness for a stakeholder. Function is ascribed to the artefact by establishing a teleological connection between a human's goals and the artefact's behaviour. The particular functions of an artefact are ontologically independent of whether the artefact's structure is conceptualised as a physical product, a software product or a process. For example, the functions "wake people up", "be reliable" and "be punctual" may be ascribed to relevant behaviours of a mechanical alarm clock (i.e., a physical product), a virtual alarm clock (i.e., software), or a set of tasks (i.e., a process).

Artefacts are realised by processes that transform a set of "raw materials" (input) into final artefacts (output). This is in contrast to the widely held view of realisation as transforming artefact models into "real" artefacts. While it is true that realisation is guided by artefact models and other (represented) instructions, what this process ultimately transforms is only the "real" world (or "target" world – the world in which the artefact is intended to be used). Table 1 presents three specific realisation processes from the domains of mechanical engineering, software engineering and business processes. It shows that business processes are realised by transforming the potential capabilities of individual people, organisations or services (as "raw materials") into a coherent set of "actual" activities that compose the business process.

One of the specificities of processes, not shown in Table 1, is that realisation time is almost identical with use time. This means that the (use-related) functions of a realised instance of the process artefact come into effect during, or upon completion of the final step of, its realisation. This is different in the domains of mechanical and software engineering, where the use time of artefacts commences well after their realisation time, and not until a number of post-realisation activities, such as packaging, delivering and installing, are completed. We will return to this difference later.

Table 1. Three domain-specific views of realisation.

	Mechanical engineering	Software engineering	Business processes
Common name	Assembly, manufacturing	Program execution	Process enactment
Embodiment	Physical world	Computational world	Business world
Input	Physical materials and components	Computing platform	Capabilities of people, organisations, services
Output	Physical products	Software products	Business processes
Transformer	People and machines (e.g., drills, lathes, assembly robots)	Virtual machines, interpreters	People, organisations, services

3. DESIGNING

Designing comprises activities that aim at producing representations of artefacts given a set of requirements. We propose three distinct concerns in designing (Kannengiesser 2009a): architecture, implementation and adaptation.

3.1. Architecture

The notion of architecture in traditional design domains such as building design and (physical) product design (Ulrich 1995) has long been used to inspire approaches to defining architecture in software engineering. Here, architecture is commonly understood as comprising a set of components, their relationships, and the rationale oriented to various functional and non-functional requirements and constraints (Perry and Wolf 1992). Central in the representation of software architecture is the use of multiple views to allow for various forms of analysis (Kruchten 1995; Bass et al. 2003). Process architecture has been defined in similar ways. Here, the components and their relationships usually represent interconnected activities and deliverables (Browning 2009), which is consistent with the notion of structure in the FBS ontology. In the business process domain, the notion of process architecture is often understood to comprise the fundamental components that are "essential" for the operations of a specific organisation (Ould 1997; Dietz 2006). Various views have been proposed to account for different process requirements and analysis goals (Curtis et al. 1992; Scheer 2000; Browning 2009).

There are two principal motivations for specifying architectures. One motivation is to obtain high-level, descriptive models of artefacts that allow for easy comprehension and reuse of essential design concepts. The other motivation is to provide constraints for managing changes or variations across different use or realisation environments. The latter is the basis for generating multiple instances of artefacts based on the same fundamental architecture (Jiao and Tseng 2000; Bosch 2000).

3.2. Implementation

Implementation is a process that transforms an architecture (input) into a prescriptive model of the realisation process (output). This model includes very detailed descriptions of the realisation steps, and is presented in a form that can be understood by the realisation transformer (see Table 1). Table 2 shows three specific implementation processes from the domains of mechanical engineering, software engineering and business processes. They are all embodied in a represented world (which may be computational, paper-based or mental) rather than in the target world.

Table 2. Three domain-specific views of implementation.

	Mechanical engineering	Software engineering	Business processes
Common name	Assembly planning, manufacturing planning	Programming	Workflow modelling
Embodiment	Represented world	Represented world	Represented world
Input	Product architecture	Software architecture	Process architecture
Output	Assembly plans, manufacturing plans	Source code	Workflow model
Transformer	Production planner	Programmer	Workflow modeller

The output of implementation, in this chapter called the "realisation model", may be more or less similar to its input (i.e., the architecture) depending on the specific domain. In mechanical engineering, assembly and manufacturing plans are procedural (or process-based) and thus very different from corresponding product architectures that are object-based. (This is despite the fact that the basis of assembly plans is established by mapping every product component onto an individual "assembly step".) In software engineering, the way in which source code is structured is often very similar to the corresponding software architecture. For example, classes in object-oriented source code often map onto components in the software architecture. In process domains including business processes, there is a very high similarity between business process architectures and their corresponding workflow models. This is because both are process-based, and most activities in the process architecture can be mapped onto activities in the realisation model.

Implementation is not a routine, mechanistic process but an instance of designing, with the realisation process (represented in the realisation model) being the artefact. The implementer needs to create the realisation model in consideration of a variety of additional requirements and constraints related to the realisation environment. Some of these requirements and constraints may not be explicitly specified in the architecture but are constructed from the implementer's experience and interactions.

3.3. Adaptation

Adaptation refers to the activities needed for modifying the structure of a process, to respond to changed requirements or constraints. The structure to be adapted may be of the process architecture or of the realisation of that process architecture. An important class of changes that require adaptation are related to unexpected events that may occur in the realisation environment. Adaptation is then concerned with recovering instances of the realisation process to mitigate possible undesired effects. This can be done by adding or removing realisation activities, re-sequencing activities, or re-allocating resources (agents) to activities. Adaptation can be viewed as an instance of re-designing (Kannengiesser and Zhu 2010).

Take a manufacturing process of mechanical products; this process often needs to be adapted in response to variations in product demand, cost constraints, required capacity utilisation or unexpected machine breakdowns. This results in a re-designed structure of the manufacturing process, by modifying the possible kinds of manufacturing steps, their order, and the allocation of specific machines. In software engineering, source code often needs to be adapted due to unexpected faults, security threats or underperforming resources. This leads to a re-designed realisation structure in terms of modified source code fragments, e.g. by introducing new exception handlers, modifying access control, or reconfiguring interactions between program components. In process domains including business processes, workflows need to be adapted to unexpected events and new constraints, such as order cancellations, service interruptions and changed business rules (e.g., introduce fast-tracked handling of complaints from gold customers). The resulting changes in the workflow may include the addition of activities (e.g., cancel shipment) and the re-allocation of resources (e.g., alternative service, and higher-rank officer in complaint department).

Changes may be temporary, affecting only one or very few instances, or persistent with longer-term effects on the realisation process. No matter what timeframe and scope, all changes lead to re-represented workflow models, which are either mental models formed by the agents performing the realisation process (in which case the changes are viewed as runtime or *ad hoc* changes), or formal "master" models from the implementers (in which case the changes are viewed as design-time or "planned" changes). Agents performing the adaptation are either human or computational. If the agent is computational, the adaptation is commonly termed "self-adaptation".

4. ISSUES IN CURRENT PROCESS MODELS

The three concerns presented in this chapter have not been well understood in business process modelling. One reason for this is the identical, procedural style of representing architecture, realisation models and adaptation. Their components are conceptualised as activities that all look the same (see Section 3.2). Another reason is the non-persistent nature of process artefacts, and their overlapping realisation and use times (see Section 2). Architecting, which focuses on processes at use time, and implementation, which focuses on processes at realisation time, thus tend to produce identical models even though they are to describe different processes.

This Section presents how issues of complexity and flexibility can arise from an insufficient understanding of the notions of business process architecture, implementation and adaptation. As an example, we use a simplified model of a property valuation process in the Australian mortgage industry, represented as a BPMN (Business Process Modeling Notation) diagram in Figure 1.

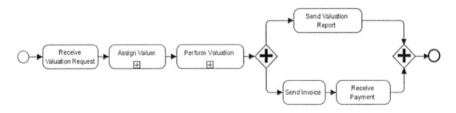

Figure 1. Property valuation process.

Here, the property valuation process (short: valuation process) starts when the valuation company receives a valuation request from a lender (e.g., a bank). A specific person (called the "valuer") is then assigned to perform the valuation by inspecting the property and preparing a valuation report that contains the estimated market value of the property. After that, the valuation report is sent to the lender, and, concurrently, an invoice is sent. Upon receipt of payment, the valuation process terminates.

This process example is quite simple; however, it is easy to see how the issues to be outlined in this Section would scale up for more detailed business process models.

4.1. Complexity

Processes are often conceptualised as paths (or sets of interrelated paths based on specified conditions) along the dimension of time. Different steps within a path are activated at different times, and their activations "flow" down the specified network of paths. This view is reflected in the term "workflow", and is consistent with the prescriptive, instructional stance inherent in realisation models. On the other hand, it is recognised that the design of processes is driven by various goals, ranging from business or organisational goals to technological constraints and quality concerns. All these aspects map onto the notions of function and behaviour that are reflected in process architectures. However, most business process specification languages, such as BPMN, EPC (Event-Driven Process Chain) and YAWL (Yet Another Workflow Language), capture only the structure aspect of processes, using (mostly graph-based) constructs to represent flows and activities. Few approaches propose representations of process goals in addition to process structure (Lapouchnian et al. 2007).

The strong similarity between process architectures and realisation models has led to their conflation and the common practice of merging them in a single process model. This may be convenient in some cases, but can cause a number of issues, one of which is complexity. We use the number of components (nodes) and their relationships (arcs) in a process model as a measure for complexity, as they have been shown to be the predominant model characteristics affecting comprehensibility (Mendling et al. 2007). A frequent cause for increased complexity is the inclusion of the fine-grained details of realisation models in process architectures. For example, activities of communication may be necessary for coordinating the people, departments or services that carry out the realisation process. However, these activities are typically not relevant on the architectural level. This has the effect that the essential, value-adding activities that form the process architecture are obscured by a multitude of ancillary realisation activities.

The complexity of many process models and their concomitant poor comprehensibility is a well-known issue in business process modelling practice. However, this issue is often perceived as a visualisation problem (Bandara et al. 2007) rather than a methodological problem. Currently, the main approach to reducing complexity is the use of hierarchical process structures that chunk some of the detailed activities into sub-processes. This is essentially an information-hiding approach. The problem here is that the complete set of sub-process attributes are hidden, including those that are needed for understanding the distinguishing nature of the specific realisation model.

For example, the "Assign Valuer" and "Perform Valuation" activities in Figure 1 are represented as "collapsed" sub-processes (indicated by the "plus" sign in the lower centre of their shapes). Figure 2 expands the "Assign Valuer" sub-process in a separate diagram, now showing all its finer-grained (realisation) details. What are the fundamental characteristics of this realisation process that distinguish them from alternative ways of realising "Assign Valuer"? One such alternative way is shown in Figure 3. Here, a bidding-style mechanism is introduced to quickly identify those potential valuers that are currently located near the property to be valuated. This mechanism is inspired by the way taxi companies dynamically assign their taxis to specific jobs. The essential differences between the alternative processes in Figures 2 and 3 can be viewed respectively as a slower, "top-down" versus a faster, self-organising realisation strategy. This higher-level, semantic characterisation is lost in simple information hiding.

Figure 2. "Assign Valuer" sub-process option 1.

Figure 3. "Assign Valuer" sub-process option 2.

4.2. Flexibility

Over-specifying realisation models as sub-processes of process architectures has the additional drawback that there is no room for local variations based on the specific constraints imposed by the realisation environment. This is because architecture, implementation and adaptation are not treated as separate activities that address separate design concerns. Once process architectures are specified that subsume all the details of the associated realisation models, there is almost no flexibility remaining. Take the activity "Assign Valuer" as an example; here, current process modelling notations such as BPMN require a particular sub-process to be defined and associated with this activity. No decision support is provided for this modelling task.

While this issue may be solved by providing meta-data, in many cases dynamic variations are required that need to be based on information captured in the process model itself. These dynamic variations are commonly known as exception handling. Here, all possible situations and events that may interfere with the process are anticipated, and ways are defined in which the process may best deal with these events. A typical example of exception handling in processes is the occurrence of an error within an activity (e.g., a system failure) or some other abnormal situation, and the definition of an additional path within the process that handles that error or abnormal situation (e.g., by repeating the process step, or by allocating the step to a different performer).

Generally, there are no reasons against using this approach. However, in many process domains it is hard if not impossible to reliably predict all possible exceptions that may occur and pre-define appropriate exception-handling strategies. In addition, the "firing" of exceptions depends on whether or not they are actively monitored for and with what techniques of sensing and analysis. These are concerns of process adaptation rather than process architecture.

Figure 4 shows an example of exception handling within the sub-process "Perform Valuation". It handles cases in which a particular valuation turns out to be difficult due to complicated site conditions, such as irregular building shapes or slopes. The valuer can generally recognise this situation upon initial visual inspection of the site. The exception is then handled by renegotiating (higher) fees with the lender. According to the exception-handling path represented in Figure 4, the renegotiation requires the valuer to go back and forth between office and property, before resuming the normal flow of activities, including performing the full inspection and preparing the valuation report.

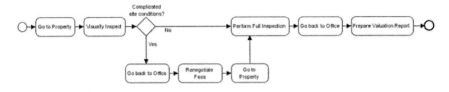

Figure 4. "Perform Valuation" sub-process option 1.

However, this is not the only way in which valuers can handle the same exception. Figure 5 shows that fee renegotiation can also be performed at a later stage within the process. This has the advantage that the valuer does not have to do the additional return trip between office and property (as in Figure 4), which can significantly speed up the valuation.

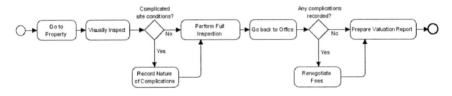

Figure 5. "Perform Valuation" sub-process option 2.

Which of the two exception-handling strategies are selected must be specified *a priori*. This restricts the valuers' freedom to flexibly decide which of the alternatives is more appropriate in the specific situation. It is certainly possible to combine both exception-handling paths into one model, Figure 6.

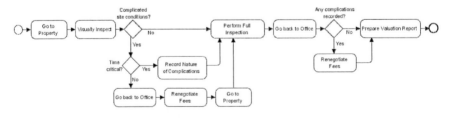

Figure 6. "Perform Valuation" sub-process option 3 (a "combination" of options 1 and 2).

However, the usefulness of such a combination is questionable, as the conditions for each path cannot be pre-defined in a sufficiently precise and complete way. Moreover, it is often cumbersome to represent multiple, intertwined paths using traditional flowchart-based notations.

The explicit representation of exception-handling, and associated mechanisms for analysing and evaluating the effect of events on the current process instance, subsumes adaptation activities in the realisation model. In other words, activities of (re-) designing are merged with the artefact. This not only adds to complexity but also makes the process inflexible by limiting the range of possible process changes to those that have been anticipated and pre-defined.

5. TOWARDS A FEATURE-BASED APPROACH

In this Section, we will present our approach to specifying concise architectures for flexible business processes, based on the "feature" concept in engineering design (Salomons et al. 1993; Shah and Mäntylä 1995). This concept is more general than the software engineering notion of features (as pieces of functionality that are of value to the customer). Features in engineering design describe any portion of an artefact's FBS representation that is significant in a particular life-cycle context (Brown 2004). For example, materials in mechanical engineering design can be viewed as features, as they are typically specified in terms of those of their FBS properties that are significant for manufacturing and use. Take this material feature labelled according to the DIN EN 10027 norm:

G-S275

This label represents cast structural steel ("G" stands for "cast"; "S" stands for "steel") with yield strength of 275 N/mm^2. It can be interpreted as an explicit specification of the function, behaviour and structure of material:

- Function: "provide the input for casting processes"
- Behaviour: yield strength ≥ 275 N/mm^2
- Structure: structural type = steel

This example demonstrates two roles of features:

1) Features as high-level building blocks: The FBS description provides high-level, semantic information rather than a low-level description of the material's molecular structure. Structure is referred to only through a label denoting its type ("steel"), based on its commonly known definition as a ferrous alloy with carbon content of less than 2.06%. Semantics is added by function and behaviour, as they provide the information relevant to product designers and product manufacturers using the material. The benefit of this representation is that it conveys rich information using a shorthand label.

2) Features as design constraints: The feature provides a set of constraints for the selection of material from a materials database. The feature representation allows specifying only those aspects that are necessary and sufficient for the task at hand. Materials can be selected (or designed) with any attribute values or additional attributes as long as the specified constraints are satisfied. If needed, the conventions in DIN EN 10027 allow increasing the set of constraints in a systematic, standardised way. For example, "G-S275JR" denotes the same material but with the additional behaviour constraint of notched impact strength of 27 Joule at 20 °C ("J" stands for 27 Joule, "R" stands for 20 °C).

Features have the potential to provide a generic tool for specifying artefacts with reduced complexity, through their role as high-level building blocks, and increased flexibility, through their role as design constraints for designing and adaptation. The domain-independent representation based on the FBS schema allows applying this tool to any class of artefact, including business processes. Unfortunately, most business process domains do not have well-established conventions and notations for labelling the FBS properties of processes or activities. However, we can demonstrate the feasibility and usefulness of integrating the feature concept in process architectures using our valuation example. Figure 7 shows that a feature-based architecture of this process can be generated by replacing fine-grained models of realisation details with annotations of their relevant function, behaviour and (high-level) structure. In particular, the Figure shows example specifications for two features, associated with "Assign Valuer" (Feature 1) and "Perform Valuation" (Feature 2).

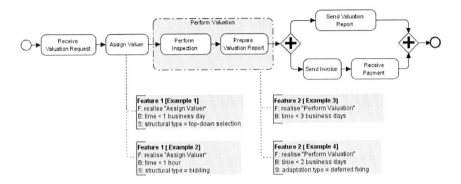

Figure 7. Feature-based architecture of a property valuation process.

Before looking more closely at the two features, note that we have chosen to represent "Perform Valuation" no longer as a sub-process (as in Figure 1) but as a loosely connected group of two core activities. This is not because we think sub-processes were generally not useful, but to emphasise that there is no one-to-one mapping between the components of process architectures and the components of their realisation. They may happen to have identical names, but they belong to fundamentally different design concerns.

The features in Figure 7 can be seen as extensions of the sub-processes in Figures 2 to 6 that are specific instances of the realisation of the valuation process. This is because the features describe relevant FBS portions of realisation that arc no longer limited to low-level details of a fixed realisation structure. For instance, the two (mutually exclusive) examples for specifying Feature 1 capture the essence of the different mechanisms for realising "Assign Valuer", in terms of their different high-level structure ("top-down" in Example 1 versus "bidding" in Example 2) and behaviour (time within 1 business day in Example 1 versus within 1 hour in Example 2). This provides a concise way of representing the relevant characteristics of the required realisation options. It also allows for more flexibility, as it makes no commitment to specific realisation details. This is in contrast to the sub-processes in Figures 2 and 3, where every activity needs to be specified explicitly.

Examples 3 and 4 for specifying Feature 2 capture alternative ways in which "Perform Valuation" can be realised. Example 3 provides a specification of the behaviour but not the structure of realisation. Here, the feature may cover any realisation structure (such as those defined in Figures 4 to 6) as long as that structure satisfies the specified behaviour. Example 4 provides a more constrained feature description, with a reduced range of possible behaviour values and a high-level specification of the mechanism required for adapting the realisation process. In this example, the adaptation mechanism is specified as "deferred fixing" that is one of the exception-handling patterns proposed by Lerner et al. (2010). The essential idea behind this pattern is that an exceptional situation is recognised and recorded, but dealt with later in the process. This fits with the sub-process in Figure 5 that records the nature of the complication but handles the consequences (i.e., the higher fees) later, after completing the full property inspection. However, this high-level pattern still allows for variations on a more detailed level. For example, one may choose to realise the activity "Renegotiate Fees" not before (as shown in Figure 5) but after preparing the valuation report.

For simplicity, our feature examples include not more than one property or constraint per ontological category. It is possible to expand the FBS descriptions as needed; for example, by adding quality attributes such as compliance, robustness and cost. As any number of constraints may be included, the reduction in process model complexity achieved through features needs to be offset against potential increases in feature complexity. However, considering that even a small number of low-level process variations can lead to highly complex process models (as illustrated in Figure 6), the use of features is very likely to reduce overall model complexity by abstracting away from structure details. Future research may investigate approaches based on distinct architectural views (Kruchten 1995; Browning 2009) to be used as information filters for cases where feature complexity becomes an issue.

We can quantify the reduction in complexity for our example. Table 3 compares the traditional and the feature-based approach based on the number of nodes (including BPMN activities, events, gateways and annotations) and arcs (including BPMN sequence flows and associations) of models of the valuation process using different combinations of realisation options. As there are two options presented for realising the "Assign Valuer" activity (Figures 2 and 3) and three options presented for realising the "Perform Valuation" activity (Figures 4, 5 and 6), we consider six combinations of options. We refer to every combination of options as a realisation instance, described as a tuple (AssignVal, PerformVal), with AssignVal and PerformVal representing specific realisation options for "Assign Valuer" and "Perform Valuation", respectively. For example, the tuple (2, 1) represents the realisation instance that uses option 2 for "Assign Valuer" (Figure 3), and option 1 for "Perform Valuation" (Figure 4). The Table shows that the traditional approach requires higher numbers of nodes and arcs than the feature-based approach. This is because it includes the nodes and arcs of all the realisation details, captured as sub-processes. In contrast, the feature-based approach extracts the essence of these details and adds it as annotations to the process architecture. The resulting reduction in complexity is significant, averaging more than 50% with respect to both nodes and arcs. It can be expected that the feature-based approach can lead to even higher reductions of complexity for larger business processes.

Table 3. Complexity of traditional and feature-based models of the valuation process

Realisa-tion instance	Complexity when using traditional approach		Complexity when using feature-based approach		Reduction in complexity when using feature-based approach	
	No. of nodes	No. of arcs	No. of nodes	No. of arcs	Reduction in no. of nodes	Reduction in no. of arcs
(1, 1)	28	27	13	13	53.6%	51.9%
(1, 2)	28	28	13	13	53.6%	53.6%
(1, 3)	32	33	13	13	59.4%	60.6%
(2, 1)	27	25	13	13	51.9%	48.0%
(2, 2)	27	26	13	13	51.9%	50.0%
(2, 3)	31	31	13	13	58.1%	58.1%
Average	28.8	28.3	13	13	54.8%	53.7%

The flexibility of the feature-based approach is difficult to evaluate quantitatively. However, it can be shown qualitatively that it introduces a new class of flexibility that can be called "design freedom". It is well demonstrated by Example 3 in Figure 7, which allows for maximum design freedom by specifying requirements pertaining only to the function and behaviour of "Perform Valuation" and not its structure. Existing approaches to process flexibility have been shown to be based on specifying constraints only on structure but not behaviour and function (Kannengiesser 2009b).

6. RELATED WORK

The notions of architecture, implementation and adaptation, in the way presented in this chapter, have not previously been applied to processes. Yet, there has been some work related to the issues of complexity and flexibility in business process modelling.

A number of approaches to reducing process complexity are based on transformations of given process models. For example, graph reduction rules have been used for control-flow verification (Sadiq and Orlowska 1999). An approach by Polyvyanyy et al. (2008) identifies less significant activities in a process model based on measures of probability and effort. A new process model is then generated by either eliminating these activities or aggregating them with other activities. However, these approaches reduce model complexity without extracting and preserving higher-level semantics. This results in a potential loss of vital information for understanding, analysing and evaluating the process. Other approaches are limited to process model syntax. For example, the design structure matrix has been used as a compact schema for visualising and analysing interdependencies among activities (Browning 2002).

Process patterns (Van der Aalst et al. 2003) and process reference models (Motschnig-Pitrik et al. 2002) provide generic process descriptions that may be suited for a common ontology of higher-level realisation structures. We have demonstrated this use of a (exception-handling) pattern as part of our feature-based approach in Section 5. However, most existing patterns and reference models provide little support for reuse (Reinhartz-Berger et al. 2005).

The issue of process flexibility has been addressed by work on state space representations of processes (Regev et al. 2007). Flexibility can be understood here as the ability to move within a state space by selecting different values of the states within given ranges. Different instantiations of this concept have been proposed, including process constraints and process fragments (Sadiq et al. 2005), and parameters for individual activities within a process (Simidchieva et al. 2007). Business process modelling experts may then specify only a "core process", allowing for the late binding of values to invariants according to individual or dynamically emerging needs. However, what is missing in these approaches is the explicit consideration of goals and requirements. Their focus has thus far been on setting up and constraining the state space of process structure but not process behaviour or process function.

As a result, there is no way of specifying criteria that guide the selection of appropriate process structures.

CONCLUSION

The contributions of this chapter are twofold. First, the chapter provides a domain-independent understanding of designing and the concerns of architecture, implementation and adaptation. This understanding sheds new light on the known issues of complexity and flexibility in business process modelling. They now appear as symptoms of the more fundamental problem of separating the three design concerns.

Second, the chapter proposes the feature concept in engineering design as the basis of a general technique for specifying the relationships between the different concerns. The FBS ontology is used for systematically and uniformly representing all features. This allows specifying concise business process architectures that constrain implementation and adaptation to an extent that is necessary and sufficient for the particular goals and requirements imposed by different business process environments. Business processes that are realised based on feature-based architectures are more flexible than those based on conventional business process models. This is because business process re-designing (i.e., adaptation) is no longer in the straightjacket of a fixed process model but delegated to local, dynamic decision-making controlled by design constraints.

Our approach has the potential to drive further research in both business process modelling and software architecture. In business process modelling, we see our work as a motivator for new efforts in describing process patterns and reference models directed towards better reuse as high-level building blocks for process design. Domain ontologies need to be developed to define standards for systematic and extensible labelling of business processes that reflect their function, behaviour and structure.

Our re-conceptualisation of business process modelling also provides opportunities for developing new software engineering approaches to supporting the design, analysis and enactment of services and business processes. Specifically, software architectures are to be tailored to the different needs of the three process design concerns. A suitable basis for developing these architectures may be the FBS framework that represents all instances of designing uniformly, including architecting, implementing and adapting business processes.

ACKNOWLEDGMENTS

NICTA is funded by the Australian Government as represented by the Department of Broadband, Communications and the Digital Economy and the Australian Research Council through the ICT Centre of Excellence program.

REFERENCES

Bandara W., Indulska M., Chons S. and Sadiq S. (2007) *Major issues in business process management: An expert perspective*, BPTrends, October 2007: 1-8.

Bass L., Clements P. and Kazman R. (2003) *Software Architecture in Practice*, Addison-Wesley, Boston.

Bosch J. (2000) *Design and Use of Software Architectures: Adopting and Evolving a Product-Line Approach*, Addison-Wesley, Boston.

Brown D.C. (2004) *Features in knowledge intensive CAD: Roles & types*, in J.C. Borg, P.J. Farrugia and K.P. Camilleri (eds.) Knowledge Intensive Design Technology, Kluwer Academic Publishers, Dordrecht, pp. 53-64.

Browning T.R. (2002) *Process integration using the design structure matrix,* Systems Engineering 5(3): 180-193.

Browning T.R. (2009) *The many views of a process: Toward a process architecture framework for product development processes*, Systems Engineering 12(1): 69-90.

Curtis B., Kellner M.I. and Over J. (1992) *Process modeling, Communications of the ACM* 35(9): 75-90.

Dietz J.L.G. (2006) *Enterprise Ontology: Theory and Methodology*, Springer-Verlag, Berlin.

Dumas M., van der Aalst W.M.P. and ter Hofstede A.H.M. (eds.) (2005) *Process-Aware Information Systems: Bridging People and Software through Process Technology,* John Wiley & Sons, Hoboken.

Gero J.S. (1990) Design prototypes: *A knowledge representation schema for design*, AI Magazine 11(4): 26-36.

Gero J.S. and Kannengiesser U. (2004) *The situated function-behaviour-structure framework*, Design Studies 25(4): 373-391.

Gero J.S. and Kannengiesser U. (2007) *A function-behavior-structure ontology of processes,* Artificial Intelligence for Engineering Design, Analysis and Manufacturing 21(4): 379-391.

Jiao J. and Tseng M.M. (2000) *Fundamentals of product family architecture*, Integrated Manufacturing Systems 11(7): 469-483.

Kannengiesser U. (2009a) *Can we engineer better process models?*, International Conference on Engineering Design 2009, Stanford University, Stanford, CA, pp. 1/527-538.

Kannengiesser U. (2009b) *Process flexibility: A design view and specification schema*, in J. Mendling, S. Rinderle-Ma and W. Esswein (eds.) Enterprise Modelling and Information Systems Architectures 2009, University of Ulm, Germany, pp. 111-124.

Kannengiesser U. and Zhu L. (2010) Rationale in semi-structured processes, *1st International Workshop on Traceability and Compliance of Semi-Structured Processes*, Business Process Management 2010, Hoboken, NJ, unnumbered.

Kruchten P. (1995) *Architectural blueprints – The "4+1" view model of software architecture*, IEEE Software 12(6): 42-50.

Kruchten P. (2005) *Casting software design in the function-behavior-structure framework*, IEEE Software 22(2): 52-58.

Lapouchnian A., Yu Y. and Mylopoulos J. (2007) *Requirements-driven design and configuration management of business processes*, in G. Alonso, P. Dadam and M. Rosemann (eds.) Business Process Management 2007, Springer-Verlag, Berlin, pp. 246-261.

Lerner B.S., Christov S., Osterweil L.J., Bendraou R., Kannengiesser U. and Wise A. (2010) *Exception handling patterns for process modeling*, IEEE Transactions on Software Engineering 36(2): 162-183.

Motschnig-Pitrik R., Randa P. and Vinek G. (2002) *Specifying and analysing static and dynamic patterns of administrative processes*, in S. Wrycza (ed.) European Conference on Information Systems 2002, Gdansk, Poland, pp. 862-871.

Mendling J., Reijers H.A. and Cardoso J. (2007) *What makes process models understandable?*, in G. Alonso, P. Dadam and M. Rosemann (eds.) Business Process Management 2007, Springer-Verlag, Berlin, pp. 48-63.

Ould M.A. (1997) *Designing a re-engineering proof process architecture*, Business Process Management Journal 3(3): 232-247.

Perry D.E. and Wolf A.L. (1992) *Foundations for the study of software architecture*, ACM SIGSOFT Software Engineering Notes 17(4): 40-52.

Polyvyanyy A., Smirnov S. and Weske M. (2008) *Process model abstraction: A slider approach*, IEEE International Enterprise Distributed Object Computing Conference 2008, Munich, Germany, pp. 325-331.

Regev G., Bider I. and Wegmann A. (2007) *Defining business process flexibility with the help of invariants*, Software Process: Improvement and Practice 12(1): 65-79.

Reinhartz-Berger I., Soffer P. and Sturm A. (2005) *A domain engineering approach to specifying and applying reference models,* in J. Desel, and U. Frank (eds.) Workshop Enterprise Modelling and Information Systems Architectures, Klagenfurt, Austria, pp. 50-63.

Sadiq S.W. and Orlowska M.E. (1999) *Applying graph reduction techniques for identifying structural conflicts in process models*, in M. Jarke and A. Oberweis (eds.) Advanced Information Systems Engineering, LNCS 1626, Springer-Verlag, Berlin, pp. 195-209.

Sadiq S.W., Orlowska M.E. and Sadiq W. (2005) *Specification and validation of process constraints for flexible workflows,* Information Systems 30(5): 349-378.

Salomons O.W., van Houten F.J.A.M. and Kals H.J.J. (1993) *Review of research in feature-based design,* Journal of Manufacturing Systems 12(2): 113-132.

Scheer A.-W. (2000) ARIS – *Business Process Modeling*, Springer-Verlag, Berlin.

Shah J.J. and Mäntylä M. (1995) *Parametric and Feature-Based CAD/CAM: Concepts,* Techniques, and Applications, John Wiley & Sons, New York.

Simidchieva B.I., Clarke L.A. and Osterweil L.J. (2007) *Representing process variation with a process family,* in Q. Wang, D. Pfahl and D.M. Raffo (eds.) Software Process Dynamics and Agility, LNCS 4470, Springer-Verlag, Berlin, pp. 109-120.

Ulrich K. (1995) *The role of product architecture in the manufacturing firm,* Research Policy 24(3): 419-440.

Van der Aalst W.M.P., ter Hofstede A.H.M., Kiepuszewski B. and Barros A.P. (2003) *Workflow patterns, Distributed and Parallel Databases* 14(3): 5-51.

In: Business Process Modeling
Editor: Jason A. Beckmann

ISBN: 978-1-61209-344-4
©2011 Nova Science Publishers, Inc.

Chapter 5

CONTEXT-AWARE METHODS FOR PROCESS MODELING

Karsten Ploesser and Jan Recker[*]
Queensland University of Technology

ABSTRACT

Recent studies have started to explore context-awareness as a driver in the design of adaptable business processes. The emerging challenge of identifying and considering contextual drivers in the environment of a business process are well understood, however, typical methods used in business process modeling do not yet consider this additional contextual information in their process designs. In this chapter, we describe our research towards innovative and advanced process modeling methods that include mechanisms to incorporate relevant contextual drivers and their impacts on business processes in process design models. We report on our ongoing work with an Australian insurance provider and describe the design science we employed to develop these innovative and useful artifacts as part of a context-aware method framework. We discuss the utility of these artifacts in an application in the claims handling process at the case organization.

Keywords: process design, design science, context-awareness

[*] {k.ploesser; j.recker}@qut.edu.au

1. INTRODUCTION

Recent studies have explored 'context-awareness' (Rosemann, Recker, & Flender, 2008) as a new paradigm in designing and managing business processes. This paradigm is grounded in the observation that business processes are coupled with elements in their external context (e.g., weather patterns, commodity prices, or industrial actions). For example, an Australian agency handling disaster claims had to apologize to victims of the Victorian bushfire in 2009 after automated letters were sent out, demanding that they provide identification, despite the fact that many of them had lost all proof of identification in the inferno (Maher, 2009). In another example, a German bank lost €300 million in an automated swap transaction with its business partner, Lehman Brothers, on the day the American investment bank announced bankruptcy (Moore, 2008). As a result of coupling, processes need to rapidly adapt if their context changes.

The requirement for rapid, context-driven adaptation, however, has not yet found its way into typical approaches for business process modeling (Rosemann, Recker, Flender, & Ansell, 2006). This is because typical methods of process modeling do not yet consider context variables but instead focus on articulating internal process viewpoints such as transformation, events or decompositions (Recker, Rosemann, Indulska, & Green, 2009). As we will show, this internally focused viewpoint creates several challenges in practice. We contend, therefore, that there is a lack of concrete artifacts to support the 'context-aware' process modeler in adapting processes to a changing context.

This chapter reports on the design and application of artifacts to support context-aware process modeling. Based on a case study with an Australian insurance provider, we explore limitations of traditional modeling approaches and derive two key requirements for innovative artifacts that extend classical process modeling. We describe the nature and type of these artifacts and conclude by demonstrating the application of the artifacts to a scenario in the case study.

2. A MOTIVATING EXAMPLE

Consider in the following our case study work with an Australian insurance company (Ploesser, Recker, & Rosemann, 2010). Since 2008, the insurer has been exposed to a string of natural disasters while investment returns have been diminishing in the global financial crisis. The constant pressure on its claims organization and claims handling & fulfillment processes has had an adverse effect on the insurer's profitability.

For each loss incurred and reported, the insurer needs to balance grade of service, indemnity cost, and claims handling expenses. Under normal circumstances, the 'claims process system' (i.e., the organizational and technical components of the claims organization) is calibrated to handle losses as efficient and effective as possible. This is achieved by a set of controls (e.g., what proofs are requested from the insured, which policy limits are to be applied, etc.) and according processes (e.g., 'no-touch', 'light-touch', and 'case-managed').

However, the claims process system is not static but needs to be recalibrated for each different 'context' in which losses are incurred (e.g., global financial crisis, Victorian bushfires, Sydney sandstorms, Queensland floods, etc.). This has two reasons. Firstly, disasters require the insurer to handle different volumes in different timeframes (e.g., numerous moderate losses in the weeks following a storm, few major losses over months after bushfires). Secondly, each disaster exposes the insurer to different types of leakage (i.e., inflated payouts) or opportunistic fraud (e.g., the risk of fraud differs between rural and urban areas).

In the case interviews, respondents provided a narrative of decisions taken to adapt the process in different contexts and recurring issues they observed. In the interest of brevity, we refer the reader to our extensive case analysis in (Ploesser, Janiesch, Recker, & Rosemann, 2009; Ploesser et al., 2010). Table 6 summarizes some of the contextual factors we identified as root causes for changes within the claims handling business processes. In Table 6, the noted business effects are linked to events occurring in the context of the organization, and also linked to resulting process change.

Table 6. Case observations.

Observed Effect	Context Variable	Example for Process Change
Changes in complexity of losses incurred	Weather event	Changes in call centre script
Changes in the loss volume incurred	Weather event	Changes in call centre rostering and overtime
Changes in the cost of replacement	Inflation	Changes to quotation process for replacement
Hiring freeze	Economic cycle	Reassignment of staff from other departments (e.g., sales)

As can be seen from Table 6, our case presents several situations in which the demand to include an environmental element such as weather (e.g., storm) as a contextual variable in a process model is prevalent in order to select and execute the correct process scenario. We would argue that process models should facilitate an understanding of exactly such cause-effect relationships between environmental events and resulting process change as summarized in Table 6.

Yet, traditionally, process models are disconnected from the relevant context in which they are valid and there is often no traceability to the situation in which the process should take place (Rosemann *et al.*, 2008). A workaround that can often be observed in modeling practice is that relevant contextual variables become an explicit part of the control flow, leading to a decision point such as "Check, if process occurs within storm season". Yet, such a workaround leads to unnecessary model extensions, mixes individual run-time with build-time decisions and tends to reduce the acceptance of the process models by end users who would not be exposed to this decision in the daily execution of the process. A second commonly employed workaround is to design multiple process models for different scenarios (e.g., for different countries) and to highlight process deviations within these models (e.g., by color coding). The shortcoming of this approach is the high degree of redundancy between the models. Figure 28 shows how such a workaround could look like for our motivating case.

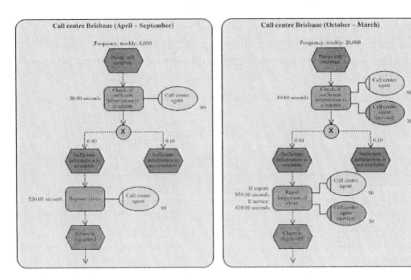

Figure 28. Context-driven process modeling workarounds (Rosemann et al., 2008).

In summary, our motivating case shows how a change in the environment requires flexible process adaptation. A process model should be linked to its relevant context in order to be able to select the applicable model so that there is a direct relationship between context and the way the process is executed and the selection of the organizational resources. This change can then be anticipated and triggered when the relevant change occurs (e.g. a change in weather). The knowledge of the cause effect chain (for example: storm season begins $\rightarrow$ more damages $\rightarrow$ increased volume of claims $\rightarrow$ increased call pick up time $\rightarrow$ increased process costs) should, therefore be made explicit in the process designs. Current process modeling techniques, however, provide only little support for modeling the relevant stimuli for change or the cause-effect relationships to the process.

In the following, we report on our design science work towards context-aware methods that assist in identifying, documenting and analyzing contextual elements relevant to business processes.

We believe a context-aware method framework will help to better understand the interrelationships between changes in the relevant environmental setting of an organization and the imposed process changes. Overall, such contextualized process landscapes can provide an efficient source for impact analyses. The potential benefits are improved process modifications (as described in our example), better risk assessments or more agile process executions.

3. CONTEXT-AWARE METHODS TO SUPPORT PROCESS MODELING

3.1 Preliminaries

The context taxonomy introduced by Rosemann et al. (2008) provides the underlying frame for our research. It introduces a stratified model of business process context encompassing immediate, internal, external, and environmental variables affecting business process execution. In the context of process modeling, it can be used to capture, group, and classify relevant (internal and external) process variables. However, the stratified context model does not specify concrete guidelines for the creation of context-aware business process models based on the context taxonomy.

Through our research on context-dependent processes in several industries (Ploesser et al., 2009; Ploesser et al., 2010; Rosemann & Recker, 2006; Rosemann et al., 2008), we identified three key challenges that arise in the context-aware modeling of business processes. Process managers and business analysts responsible for the design and operation of context-dependent processes require an understanding of:

a)   what are relevant context variables in the external environment of the firm,
b)   where do such variables affect its business process, and
c)   how do changes in context variables affect business process performance.

Business process modeling is an approach used to specify the internal structure and (observable) behavior of business processes. Business processes are typically represented as chronological sequences of events that occur during the transformation of an input (e.g., a customer request) into an output (e.g., a finished good or service provided by the firm). Most existing process modeling methods provide support for specifying the most important immediate and internal variables, viz., control flow, data, application, and resources pertaining to a business process (Scheer, 2000).

Table 7 provides an overview of process variables commonly supported in popular process modeling methods. It follows the layers provided by the stratified context model developed by Rosemann et al. (2008). In this table, a "+" indicates a direct support for a context element, a "+/–" indicates a partial support and a "–" indicates a lack of support. Extended EPCs, for instance, provide a means to integrate data models with process models and as such provide explicit and comprehensive support for the data perspective in process models. BPMN, on the other hand, restricts its support for the articulation of process-related data to the modeling of 'Data Objects'. Yet, no information about data structure, data types or data relationships can be articulated. Thus, BPMN's support for this perspective is only partial. We found no noticeable support for the specification of external variables in process modeling with the exception of risk annotations (Rosemann & zur Muehlen, 2005).

Realizing that common process modeling methods do not provide adequate support to model contextual variables, we turn to techniques originating in the management sciences and operations research to model the external and environmental context variables of business processes. The study of extraneous variables and their impact on operations has long been of interest to operations researchers. Forrester (1994) and Sterman's (2000) work on industrial dynamics, for instance, views processes as complex systems of multiple, interlocked components that interact closely with their external environment. Tight coupling and feedback loops between endogenous and/or exogenous system variables gives rise to complex behavior over time.

Table 7. Popular process modeling methods and supported context layers.

Method	Immediate/internal				External/ envtl.
	Control	Data	Application	Resource	
eEPC	+	+	+	+	-
BPMN	+	+/-	+/-	+	-
Petri Nets	+	-	-	-	-
IDEF3	+	+/-	-	-	-
YAWL	+	+	+/-	+	-
UML AD	+	+	-	+/-	-

Based on this viewpoint of processes as complex systems, System Dynamics (SD) modeling (e.g., Sterman, 2000) was developed to help managers understand the behavior of complex (industrial) systems and their evolution over time. An SD model recreates the structure and dynamics of a system (e.g., a production process) as a set of aggregate variables (stocks), rates of processing (flows), and feedback loops. As such it is able to capture the interaction of variables in the external and environmental context of a firm with the internal structure of its business processes. However, SD in its original form provides no built-in integration into common process modeling standards.

3.2 Global and Local Views on Processes

To remediate the missing support for context specification in contemporary process modeling methods, we propose a multi-viewpoint approach that combines the features of process and SD modeling. Multi-viewpoint modeling (Avison & Wood-Harper, 1990), i.e., the representation of different aspects of a common problem using separate 'views', is a technique often used in conceptual modeling to facilitate the specification of complex problems. For example, consider the dedicated viewpoints defined in UML 2.0 (i.e., the differentiation into structural and behavioral diagram types) and

BPMN 2.0 (e.g., the choreography and orchestration diagrams pertaining to a BPMN 2.0 model).

In extension to the 'local' viewpoint supported by most process modeling methods (cf. Table 7), we define a 'global' viewpoint detailing the interaction between process variables and environmental variables. A process model therefore comprises a set of endogenous (i.e., inventories) and exogenous variables (i.e., context variables). In this view, activities move quantities between inventories. Context variables in turn affect the 'level' of these inventories, the characteristics of their 'content', and the ability of activities to move an expected quantity between inventories. For example, the occurrence of the factor 'storm' rapidly fills the claim inventory of an insurance carrier with claims of higher-than-average complexity. Simultaneously, it may limit the process activity of 'claim adjustment' as claim adjustment capacity is limited.

The global viewpoint of the process is a 'causally closed' model of external and internal process variables and the dynamics of their interaction. The according diagram specifies how changes in an exogenous variable (weather, consumer price index) affect endogenous process variables (e.g. claims inflow, adjusting resources, repair cost), taking into consideration time delays. There is a comprehensive body of literature (e.g., Forrester, 1994) on issues dealing with the identification, creation, and communication of such models. The purpose of this diagram is to provide management with an overview of important process variables and their principal feedback structure.

Figure 29 shows the principal elements of the global view diagram using stock & flow notation as defined by Sterman (2000). Rectangles represent the principal inventories of the process. Valves depict the flow rate between inventories. Arrows connect inventories with rates to specify that information (about flow objects such as insurance claims) is flowing between them. Exogenous variables connect to rates or inventories and specify the (quantifiable) impact of context change on either one. Consider a simple order handling process. The order volume depends on the competitiveness of the firm's pricing and availability of substitute products.

The local viewpoint, on the other hand, defines in detail the activities undertaken by the firm to produce an output. In particular, it specifies the relevant events (e.g., 'First Notice of Loss'), activities (e.g., loss adjustment), attributes of flow units (e.g., the details of an insurance claim such as the loss value and scope of work), and resources (e.g., business application, labor) required in the process of conversion. The purpose of this diagram is to inform management about which activities are executed in a business process and where context changes potentially affect business process execution.

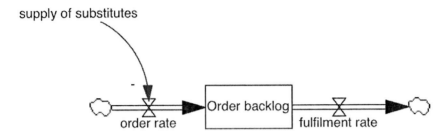

Figure 29. Example of global process view.

Figure 30 shows an excerpt of the local view of the same order handling process presented in Figure 29 using the current standard BPMN 2.0 notation. Inventories are represented as data store objects, events are described as circles, activities as rounded rectangles, and convergence and divergence semantics are described in diamond-shaped gateways. Note that context variables are not displayed on this level of detail. However, they are implicitly part of the data context of the process and may be referred to in expressions and conditions (e.g., in branching decisions contained in the diamond-shaped gateways).

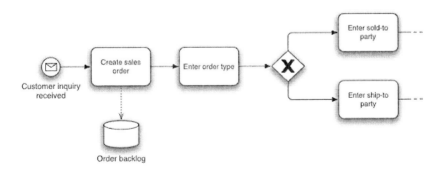

Figure 30. Example of local process view in standard BPMN 2.0 flowchart notation.

As can be seen from Figure 30, local views on processes complement the highly aggregate global view provided through SD modeling. This is achieved through added details about the events and activities that occur during processing. The local view further allows the association of activities to organizational units, resources, or application systems and the detailed specification of information flow between process participants. For more information and a detailed discussion of issues pertaining to process modeling, we point the reader to the overview provided by Indulska et al. (2009).

3.3 A Context-Aware Modeling Method

The flowchart diagram in Figure 31 renders the important decision points and activities involved in creating context-aware business process models. In section 3.1, we defined the three concerns that guide context-aware process modeling as: *what, where,* and *how* context change affects business process performance. The method presented in this section is based on, and extends, our prior research (Ploesser et al., 2009; Rosemann et al., 2008).

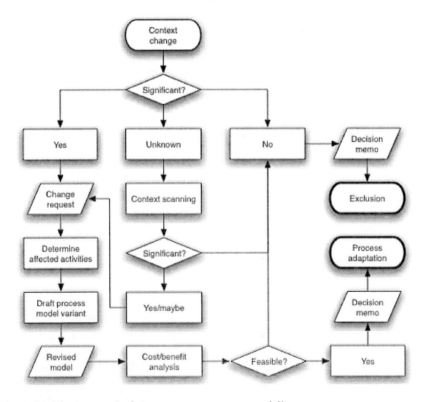

Figure 31. The 'process' of context-aware process modeling.

We begin by assessing whether a context change should be considered relevant or significant for process execution ('what'). Significance is generally measured as the cost of an impending KPI violation or opportunity cost (i.e., cost of output forgone) incurred if the process is not adapted.

In case a change was found to be significant, we determine the available process scenarios and evaluate which scenario best corresponds to the emerging situation, e.g., by mitigating negative effects on process activities ('where'). If the required process changes are feasible and the cost of implementation does not outweigh its benefits ('how'), we approve and execute the changes.

In case the significance of a context change for the business processes of a firm is unclear, additional effort is required to isolate and analyze context variables. We refer to the process in which context variables are isolated, classified, and analyzed as 'context scanning' (Ploesser et al., 2009). Context scanning may be conducted using a variety of techniques. For example, Dohmen and Moormann (2010) discuss a quantitative approaches to the discovery of 'inefficiency' drivers, that corresponds to our notion of 'context variable'.

4. AN ILLUSTRATION OF THE ARTIFACTS

Let us apply these artifacts to the problem of the case study presented above. Natural disasters trigger spikes in claims volume that require the insurer to handle more claims in less time. In response to this situation, the insurer developed a streamlined lodgment system that allows the fast capture of loss information. In a linear system (Figure 32), this should lead to an increase in the overall processing rate achieved by the insurer.

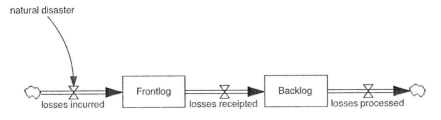

Figure 32. Context-unaware model of process chain.

However, the relationship between claims volume and settled claims in a disaster is not linear. The process is tightly coupled and any change in one component can generate flow-on effects on other components. For example, an increased lodgment rate does not result in a linear increase in the overall processing rate. Instead, the overall processing rate falls below expectations, due to the lack of context-awareness in the model shown in Figure 32.

Figure 33 extends Figure 32 by feedback loops. These feedback loops depict how pressure slowly builds up after a disaster as a result of a spike in volume and heightened attention. The streamlined lodgment process, once activated, requires the claims handler in the 'front-end' to spend less time in handling a call and to capture less information about the loss cause. However, the time gained is lost later in the 'back-end' of the process. Claims handlers now spend increasing time in recovering the missing information and handling return calls from disgruntled customers. This ultimately slows the overall processing capacity.

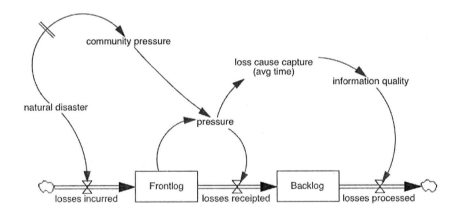

Figure 33. Context-extended model of process chain.

Next, we model the process activities from the time the first notice of loss is received (the 'frontlog') to the time the claim is passes to the 'backend' for settlement (the 'backlog'). We then integrate the feedback structure modeled in the previous step. Purpose of this exercise is to trace the flow of information and identify those activities that contribute to the problem.

Figure 34 shows the activities conducted by claims handlers in the 'front-end' of the process. In this model, it is possible to revert back to established process modeling methods. In our case, we follow the BPMN 2.0 notation (OMG, 2009), the current industry standard for process modeling (Recker,

2010). Note that the concept of system inventory is mapped to the concept of 'data store' as defined by version 2.0 of BPMN.

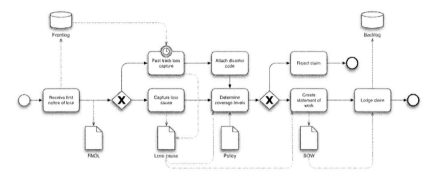

Figure 34. Integrating feedback structure and process model.

5. DISCUSSION

Our case findings and the outcomes of our design research cycle suggest a high relevance of the concepts 'context-awareness' and 'context-driven process adaptation'. We provided a motivating example in which business processes of an insurance carrier encounter different situations (e.g., business as usual, storm, hail, flooding), sometimes even simultaneously (c.g., processing normal losses and natural disaster losses in parallel).

We attributed these different situations to changes in external variables of the process and showed that processes need to be rapidly re-calibrated each time the context changes (e.g., decreased business volume during economic slowdown, increased probability of weather incidents during Australian storm or bushfire season). This change requires all stakeholders in the affected business processes (e.g., management, staff, and suppliers) to have a mutual understanding of the factors that determine a certain situation, of the impact these factors have on their actions, and how they must adapt their behavior for their work to be productive and profitable in the new situation.

By applying the approach described in this chapter, we demonstrated how the introduction of global and local process views enables a much more comprehensive representation of context-dependent business processes than traditional modeling techniques such as EPC or BPMN. These arguments have implication for the design and implementation of business processes. We argue that organizations need to address three challenges to increase the adaptiveness of business processes:

a)   discovering and understanding context,
b)   analyzing the impact of context change, and
c)   enforcing corrective action.

We suggest that the context-aware modelling method proposed in this article will enable firms to analyse and optimise business processes in different contexts. As part of this, we see the need to scan and monitor relevant variables in the external context of the business processes. Environmental scanning (Aguilar, 1967) has been used to some effect in long range strategic planning, but is typically on a broader level of abstraction and covers a more long term time horizon. An alternative could consist of the development of key context indicators, similar to performance (e.g., Soffer & Wand, 2005) and risk indicators used in process management today (e.g., Rosemann & zur Muehlen, 2005).

Similarly, we argued the need for the inclusion of context variables into the business process management lifecycle. The consideration of context variables in the analysis, design, and implementation stages of the lifecycle can support firms in identifying the need for adaptiveness and defining suitable adaptation strategies along the process chain. This information may then also be used to guide investments into suitable ERP platforms.

The challenges we discussed and the need for context-aware process modelling also suggest new opportunities for researchers to develop appropriate technologies to discover and analyse variables in the process context as well as to provide decision support for identifying corrective action. Some related work exists in the research streams of process configuration, workflow management, and process flexibility. La Rosa et al. (2009) present an approach that captures system variability based on questionnaire models and supports the modelling of order dependencies and domain constraints. Hallerbach et al. (2010) discuss the context-based definition and configuration of process variants by applying a set of well-defined change operations to a reference process model. Finally, Weber et al. (2007) introduce a method to develop process-based systems that support users in reusing adaptation 'patterns' that proved successful in similar contexts.

However, to date, these contributions rely on a fixed set of parameters and adaptation rules (Hallerbach et al., 2010; La Rosa et al., 2009) or use unstructured text to capture contextual information after an adaptation decision was made (Weber *et al.*, 2007), and need further extensions towards truly flexible context-awareness.

CONCLUSION

In a networked, tightly coupled environment, organizations need to prepare for rapid, context-driven adaptation of business processes. Following a review of popular process modeling methods, we argued that process modeling so far has several shortcomings with respect to modeling context-aware business processes. In particular, we highlight the missing link between context variables (i.e., factors in the external environment of the firm) and business process scenarios (i.e., alternative ways of executing the process).

We demonstrated how extending process modeling using dedicated context-aware artifacts expands the modeling viewpoint such that the models can capture the feedback between *external* and *internal* process variables and thus gain an enhanced understanding of the behavior of the process in relation to the context in which it operates. We introduced a process modeling approach that provides two viewpoints, the global feedback structure of the process and the local process description itself.

The two viewpoints introduced above therefore act as explanatory devices to describe the coupling between context and process and to explain the resulting behavior. On basis of such modeling, managers and analysts are provided with a deeper understanding and more transparent articulation of a business process within the context it operates.

REFERENCES

Aguilar, F. J. (1967). *Scanning the Business Environment*. New York, New York: MacGraw-Hill.

Avison, D. E., & Wood-Harper, A. T. (1990). *Multiview: An Exploration in Information Systems Development*. Maidenhead, England: McGraw Hill.

Dohmen, A., & Moormann, J. (2010). *Identifying Drivers of Inefficiency in Business Processes: A DEA and Data Mining Perspective*. In I. Bider, T. A. Halpin, J. Krogstie, S. Nurcan, E. Proper, R. Schmidt & R. Ukor (Eds.), Enterprise, Business-Process and Information Systems Modeling: 11th International Workshop, BPMDS 2010, and 15th International

Conference, EMMSAD 2010, held at CAiSE 2010, Hammamet, Tunisia, June 7-8, 2010 (Vol. 50, pp. 146-157). Hammamet, Tunisia: Springer.

Forrester, J. W. (1994). *System Dynamics, Systems Thinking and Soft OR.* System Dynamics Review, 10(2-3), 245-256.

Hallerbach, A., Bauer, T., & Reichert, M. (2010). *Capturing Variability in Business Process Models*: The Provop Approach. Software Process: Improvement and Practice(In Press).

Indulska, M., Recker, J., Rosemann, M., & Green, P. (2009). *Process Modeling: Current Issues and Future Challenges.* In P. van Eck, J. Gordijn & R. Wieringa (Eds.), Advanced Information Systems Engineering - CAiSE 2009 (Vol. 5565, pp. 501-514). Amsterdam, The Netherlands: Springer.

La Rosa, M., van der Aalst, W. M. P., & ter Hofstede, A. H. M. (2009). *Questionnaire-based Variability Modeling for System Configuration.* Software and Systems Modeling, 8(2), 251-274.

Maher, S. (2009). *Centrelink will apologise to victims.* The Australian.

Moore, M. S. (2008). *German Bank Under Fire for Strange Lehman Deal.* Spiegel Online.

OMG. (2009). *Business Process Modeling Notation*, V2.0. Retrieved May 31, 2010, from http://www.omg.org/spec/BPMN/2.0

Ploesser, K., Janiesch, C., Recker, J., & Rosemann, M. (2009). *Context Change Archetypes: Understanding the Impact of Context Change on Business Processes.* Paper presented at the 20th Australasian Conference on Information Systems, Melbourne, Australia.

Ploesser, K., Recker, J., & Rosemann, M. (2010). *Building a Methodology for Context-aware Business Processes: Insights from an Exploratory Case Study.* Paper presented at the 18th European Conference on Information Systems, Pretoria, South Africa.

Recker, J. (2010). Opportunities and Constraints: *The Current Struggle with BPMN.* Business Process Management Journal, 16(1), 181-201.

Recker, J., Rosemann, M., Indulska, M., & Green, P. (2009). *Business Process Modeling: A Comparative Analysis.* Journal of the Association for Information Systems, 10(4), 333-363.

Rosemann, M., & Recker, J. (2006). *Context-aware Process Design: Exploring the Extrinsic Drivers for Process Flexibility.* In T. Latour & M. Petit (Eds.), The 18th International Conference on Advanced Information Systems Engineering. Proceedings of Workshops and Doctoral Consortium (pp. 149-158). Luxembourg, Grand-Duchy of Luxembourg: Namur University Press.

Rosemann, M., Recker, J., & Flender, C. (2008). *Contextualization of Business Processes*. International Journal of Business Process Integration and Management, 3(1), 47-60.

Rosemann, M., Recker, J., Flender, C., & Ansell, P. (2006). *Context-Awareness in Business Process Design*. Paper presented at the 17th Australasian Conference on Information Systems, Adelaide, Australia.

Rosemann, M., & zur Muehlen, M. (2005). *Integrating Risks in Business Process Models*. Paper presented at the 16th Australasian Conference on Information Systems, Sydney, Australia.

Scheer, A.-W. (2000). *ARIS - Business Process Modeling* (3rd ed.). Berlin, Germany: Springer.

Soffer, P., & Wand, Y. (2005). *On the Notion of Soft-Goals in Business Process Modeling*. Business Process Management Journal, 11(6), 663-679.

Sterman, J. (2000). *Business Dynamics: Systems Thinking and Modeling for a Complex World*. Boston, Massachusetts: Irwin/McGraw-Hill.

Weber, B., Wild, W., Reichert, M., & Dadam, P. (2007). *ProCycle - Integrierte Unterstützung des Prozesslebenszyklus*. Künstliche Intelligenz Journal, 12(4), 9-15.

In: Business Process Modeling   ISBN: 978-1-61209-344-4
Editor: Jason A. Beckmann   © 2011 Nova Science Publishers, Inc.

Chapter 6

MODELING AND ANALYSIS OF BUSINESS PROCESSES WITH BUSINESS RULES

Grzegorz J. Nalepa[*], *Krzysztof Kluza*[†] *and Sebastian Ernst*[‡]
AGH University of Science and Technology, Kraków, Poland[§]

Abstract

Visual business process representation languages such as BPMN are a useful tool for specification of business processes. However, practical verification and execution of Business Process Models is a challenging task. One solution to this problem is integration of business processes with business rules, which provides a flexible runtime environment. This chapter concerns Business Process Models as a visual inference specification method for modularized rulebases. To provide the background for this approach, selected analysis and execution methods for Business Processes, such as BPEL and BPMN tools, are presented. Business Processes can be supported with Business Rules as executable logic. Rule-Based Systems have well-established methods for verification and optimization. This chapter presents selected rule-based solutions, such as Drools and XTT2 – a novel visual rule specification that provides formalized analysis – as well as their integration with BPMN as

[*]E-mail address: gjn@agh.edu.pl
[†]E-mail address: kluza@agh.edu.pl
[‡]E-mail address: ernst@agh.edu.pl
[§]The paper is supported by the BIMLOQ Project funded from 2010–2012 resources for science as a research project.

a visual method for inference specification. The proposed BPMN+XTT2 solution combines flexible business process modeling provided by BPMN with verification and execution features of XTT2.

PACS 05.45-a, 52.35.Mw, 96.50.Fm. **Keywords:** Business Process and Business Rules.

Key Words: business process, business rules AMS Subject Classification: 53D, 37C, 65P.

1. Introduction

The business process approach aims at capturing the process of an organization to achieve a business objective. With this approach specification of business systems is much simpler and more natural than with other methodologies. Visual business process representation languages such as BPMN (*Business Process Modeling Notation*) serve as a useful tool for specification of such processes. Particular kinds of work to complete some process subgoals can be described using activities such as tasks or subprocesses. Subprocesses can partly help to deal with the problem of software complexity.

A business process can be executed by a process engine. In such an engine, instances of a process can be run, if unambiguous process logic is provided. However, practical verification and execution of BPM (*Business Process Models*) is a challenging task.

One of the solutions for this problem is to transform the BPMN model to BPEL4WS (*Business Process Execution Language for Web Services*), which is an executable language used to define interaction between network services. Then, one can use tools which provide BPEL-based process simulation and analysis features.

Another solution is integration of business processes with business rules. In this case, the BPMN model specifies the behavior while rules provide a description of low-level logic. KBS (*Knowledge-Based Systems*) constitute a mature and well established technology. Specifically, RBS (*Rule-Based Systems*) are a widely-researched field. Verification, validation and testing of an RBS is already a well-studied topic [10, 11, 16]. This opens up the possibility of using one of the existing runtime environments for rules. The chapter describes both of the aforementioned solutions.

2. Business Process Implementation

The real challenge arises when it comes to designing computer systems aimed at providing complex support of all business actions, at every stage of a business process, until their completion. However, this task is related to at least two difficulties [15]:

1. Every company and organization has its own business processes and software should be adapted to the processes, not the other way round.

2. Business processes evolve as the company expands its actions. Each change would have to be reflected in the construction of the software which, in turn, would increase the costs and require very flexible software design methodologies and architectures.

The aim of creating BPMN was to standardize the bridge for the gap between business process design and implementation [14]. However, in practice, implementation of a business process is not unified. Section 3. presents an approach using BPEL4WS, and Section 4. describes a RBS-based approach to execute a business process.

3. The SOA/BPEL4WS Approach

Application of traditional software design methodologies to development of software aimed at supporting execution of business processes defined in an enterprise resulted in a semantic gap between process specification and development tools. Due to this gap, no well-defined procedures exist to reflect changes introduced in business processes during software design.

The problem is partly caused by the fact that requirements have to be specified *a priori*. Therefore, specification needs to be as precise as possible, because it determines the selection of a given software architecture. Requirements often change, either while the software is still being developed or after it has been deployed. Traditional design methodologies have not been designed with constant changes in mind. Introduction of changes into process specification requires repetition of most software lifecycle stages, which is time-consuming and expensive.

SOA (*Service Oriented Architecture*) [4, 15] tries to mitigate this problem by defining the application lifecycle from process modeling up to implementation as a working program. SOA minimizes the semantic gap between business process models and software implementing them. The basic tools of SOA are: 1) **BPMN**, a graphical notation used to model business processes. BPMN diagrams include activities and tasks within a process, as well as their relations. BPMN defines symbols used to represents activities (rectangles) or gateways (diamonds). BPMN was designed explicitly to be used for SOA applications; 2) **BPEL**, an XML-based language, used to describe business processes. Both *executable* and *abstract* processes can be described; executable processes contain all details, whether abstract ones only define message exchange between cooperating units.

Let us now proceed to the description of BPEL.

3.1.   Business Process Execution Language

WS-BPEL (full name: *Web Services Business Process Execution Language*), also referred to as BPEL or BPEL4WS, is an executable language used to define interaction between network services (*Web Services*). BPEL is based on the XML standard and allows for implementation of a SOA-based architecture [17]. Implementation of a business process using BPEL consists in arranging simple *Web Services* into more complex structures.

Simple services can be organized into complex processes based on one of two paradigms:

- the *orchestration* paradigm, which involves the existence of a coordinator, managing the execution of individual processes (Fig. 1(a)),

- the *choreography* paradigm, where no central coordinator exists, and services are 'aware' that they are part of a more complex process and handle communication with other services themselves (Fig. 1(b)).

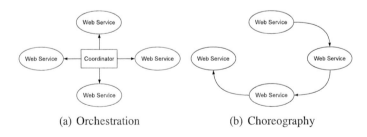

(a) Orchestration   (b) Choreography

Figure 1. Service organization paradigms (based on [17]).

In [17] two advantages of the orchestration paradigm are listed: 1) simple composite services can be included into complex business processes without the need to modify their source code; 2) possibility of implementation of alternative scenarios in case a service is unavailable.

A process model prepared using BPEL is composed of a BPEL process definition, a WSDL (*Web Services Description Language*) process specification, and files specific for the chosen execution environment.

Table 1 presents the elements within the BPEL language.

Table 1. BPEL elements

Category	Element	Description
Declarations	`<process>`	Main element.
	`<partnerLink>`	Defines parties providing services, their roles and target operations.
	`<variable>`	Data used within the process.
Simple	`<receive>`	Waits for partner's message.
	`<reply>`	Reply to partner's response.
	`<invoke>`	Invoke a partner Web Service, either as request/reply (synchronous) or one-way (asynchronous).
	`<assign>`	Copies data between variables.
	`<throw>`	Throw an exception.
	`<wait>`	Suspend activities for a given time.
	`<empty>`	Empty operation (no-op).
Structural	`<sequence>`	Execute a sequence of activities in given order.
	`<switch>`	*Case* construct.
	`<while>`	*While* loop.
	`<pick>`	Block and wait for message or alarm.
	`<flow>`	Parallel execution of a series of activities.
	`<eventHandlers>`	Receive message or alarm without blocking (process continues execution).
Management	`<scope>`	Define the scope (constraints) of variables, error handling, compensation and correlation procedures.
	`<faultHandlers>`	Define exception handling for given conditions.
	`<compensate>`	Launch compensation logic in case of error to undo previously finished activities.
	`<correlations>`	Associate messages with given process instances.
	`<terminate>`	Instantly finishes and destroys process.

3.2. BPMN to BPEL Mapping

From the modeling point of view, it is important to create visual tools allowing for convenient and clear definition of dependencies within a process. Tools used to model business processes usually take one of the following approaches:

- utilization of a known business process modeling language and translation of the semantics of its elements into BPEL elements, or

- introduction of an own graphical language, providing a better representation of the expressiveness of BPEL.

Both approaches have their pros and cons. One advantage of the second approach is an unambiguous transition from the visual model to the executable code. However, it requires the operators to learn a new language and suffers from portability problems. The first approach does not have these problems. One of the most popular languages for that purpose is BPMN.

A BPD (*Business Process Diagram*) can be composed of several partially or fully independent components, presented as separate pools. Therefore, translation into BPEL4WS applies to individual pools, rather than entire diagrams. A separate BPEL process is created for every explicitly defined (*white box*) pool. Pools defined implicitly (*black box*) also appear in BPEL schemes, e.g. as `partnerLink` elements.

The `ExpressionLanguage` and `QueryLanguage` elements are mapped into corresponding BPEL4WS elements and apply to all processes within a BPD. The `Id`, `Name`, `Version`, `Author`, `Language`, `CreationDate`, `ModificationDate`, `Pool` and `Documentation` elements are not mapped.

A BPD can contain one or more business processes – each in a separate pool. Mapping of flow control elements, events, activities, gateways and other BPMN elements has been described in detail in [14].

Work [5] indicates the fact that mapping of BPMN diagrams into BPEL processes is a difficult task, due to structural discrepancies between BPMN and BPEL. The latter has a block structure, whereas the former usually has a graph structure. Therefore, as far as structure is concerned, BPMN can be treated as a superset of BPEL. There are no basic difficulties in mapping BPEL processes into isomorphic BPMN diagrams – a BPEL process can be presented as a BPMN diagram without altering the flow structure. However, it is not always possible to translate a BPMN diagram into an isomorphic BPEL process. The freedom of control flow in BPMN can be compared to unconditional jumps

(GOTO instructions) in some programming languages. Therefore, without re-analyzing and redrawing, it may not be possible to map every BPMN process into BPEL correctly.

3.3. BPEL Tools

In real-life situations, two groups of employees are usually concerned with business process modeling: *business analysts*, who work with BPMN diagrams and try to incorporate all business requirements of the employer, and *SOA architects*, who translate process definitions into an available web service environment.

In such a modeling process, it is difficult to maintain integrity of the BPMN and BPEL models, which can be solved by employing one of the following approaches: (1) round-trip engineering, where the model is iteratively transferred between the two aforementioned groups of designers; this approach has disadvantages defined in the previous section and in [5] or (2) the synchronous approach, where full synchronization between the BPMN model and BPEL code is maintained.

BPEL definitions are used to control network services. This requires a web services infrastructure (at the design stage) or execution of processes in a production system (in case of post-deployment modifications). Therefore, it is very important to extensively test the definitions in simulation mode. Most tools allow for simulation of processes before they are launched. Three solutions have been selected for comparison:

- *eClarus Business Process Modeler* – a commercial solution, providing a very wide spectrum of functionalities, especially when used for modification of structure of existing enterprises,

- *ActiveVOS* – a commercial solution, advertised as one which supports the most recent standards (even those not yet approved),

- Eclipse-based tools: *BPMN Modeler, BPEL Editor* and the *BPMN2BPEL* converter, which are an interesting *open-source* alternative to the commercial applications.

Table 2 presents significant features of these solutions, as of June 2010.

Table 2. Feature comparison of selected applications

Feature	eClarus	ActiveVOS	Eclipse
BPMN 1.1 support	yes	yes	yes
BPMN 2.0 support	no	yes	no
BPEL 1.1 support	yes	yes	yes
BPEL 2.0 support	yes	yes	no
BPMN to BPEL translation	yes	yes	yes
BPEL to BPMN translation (BPEL scheme visualisation)	yes	yes	no
Analyst-architect cooperation type	round-trip	synchronuous	n/d
BPEL4People support	yes	yes	no
Simulation mode	yes	yes	no
Flow animation	yes	no	no
Dynamic parameter value editing	no	yes	yes
License	commercial	commercial	free

eClarus Business Process Modeler[1] is a tool aimed at business analysts, which allows for visual process design, process testing and export to executable BPEL code. Visualization of ready BPEL schemes created using other tools as BPMN diagrams is also possible. The software is based on the Eclipse platform and is available as a standalone application or an Eclipse plug-in.

ActiveVOS[2] is a business process management system, developed by Active Endpoints. The manufacturer lists the following features, distinguishing ActiveVOS from competing products: (1) Support for versions 2.0 of BPMN and BPEL, while maintaining full synchronization of the BPMN model and BPEL code, (2) Support for human-performed tasks and the BPEL4People standard including easy integration of forms as services in a business process, (3) Support for BPEL 2.0 code execution, which reduces the need for unclear adapter and connector structures (Enterprise Application Infrastructure), (4) A feature to suspend simulation, modify parameter values and resume processing.

Eclipse BPEL Editor[3] is a graphical BPEL editor, based on GEF standards. *BPML2BPEL*[4] is an open-source tool used to translate BPMN models into BPEL processes. The program is provided as an Eclipse plugin. The software does not provide BPMN modeling features – *Eclipse BPMN Modeler*[5]

[1] http://www.eclarus.com
[2] http://www.activevos.com
[3] http://www.eclipse.org/bpel/
[4] http://code.google.com/p/bpmn2bpel/
[5] http://www.eclipse.org/bpmn/

and the aforementioned *Eclipse BPEL Editor* are used for that purpose. These tools allow for one-way (BPMN to BPEL) translation. No BPEL visualization of simulation tools are provided. The functionality can be easily extended by users with programming capabilities: the editor can be supplemented with support for new activity and property types, the deployment framework allows for addition of new activities and attributes, and the validator can be supplemented with support for extension validation.

4.   Rule-Based Approaches

RBS (*Rule-Based Systems*) [10] constitute one of the most powerful knowledge representation formalisms. This approach is suitable for many kinds of computer systems. Existing solutions in the area of RBS have certain limitations. Therefore, design of complex and sophisticated rule-based systems poses difficulties. When the number of rules grows, system scalability and maintainability suffers. Moreover, the inference process would not be efficient without a proper structure and design of the rule-based system.

To avoid this, there is a need to manage rules, e.g. by grouping and hierarchization, as well as to address the contextual nature of the rulebase. Visual representation of rules can help in resolving these issues as well. However, large scale systems require a higher-level abstraction layer, which can control complexity of the system.

There are solutions which provide the means for modularization of rule bases, such as Drools Flow [3] (a popular technology for workflow or process modeling) or XTT2 (*EXtended Tabular Trees*) [12], which organizes a tabular system into a hierarchical structure. However, a new approach using BPMN (an OMG standard [14] for business process modeling) for modularization can be useful for both managing rules and modeling business process logic, as well as further analysis of a process. This section concerns a BPM as a visual inference specification method for a modularized rulebase [9].

4.1.   The XTT2 method

In the field of RBS, proper structure and design of a rule-based system is an important issue. One of the most common rule grouping methods involve context awareness and creation of decision tables. Another grouping method takes rule dependencies into account and creates decision trees, which leads to RBS modularization.

XTT2 (*EXtended Tabular Trees*) [12] is a hybrid knowledge representation and design method aimed at combining decision trees and decision tables. It uses a hierarchical visual representation of the decision tables linked into a tree-like structure. The method has been developed within the HeKatE research project (http://hekate.ia.agh.edu.pl), and its goal is to provide a new software development methodology, which tries to incorporate some well-established KE (*Knowledge Engineering*) tools and paradigms, such as declarative knowledge representation, knowledge transformation based on existing inference strategies and verification, validation and refinement, into the domain of SE (*Software Engineering*).

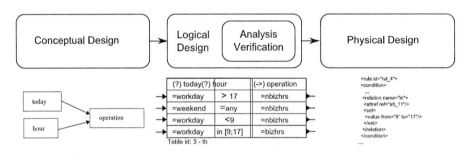

Figure 2. The HeKatE process [8].

The HeKatE process consists of three design phases (shown in Fig. 2) [12]:

1. **The conceptual design phase**, which is the most abstract one. During this phase, both system attributes and their functional relationships are identified. This phase uses ARD+ (Attribute-Relationship) diagrams as a modeling tool, which further facilitates the design of the logical XTT2 structure. However, the ARD+ method is quite simple and does not provide more advanced workflow constructs.

2. **The logical design phase**, in which the system structure is represented as a XTT2 hierarchy. The preliminary model of XTT2 can be obtained as a result of the previous phase. This phase uses the XTT2 representation as a design tool. During this phase, on-line analysis and verification, as well as revision and optimization (if necessary) of the designed system properties is provided.

3. **The physical design phase**, in which the system implementation is generated from the XTT2 model. The code is serialized in HML (*Hekate Markup Language*), an XML serialization of the HeKatE rule base, and described in the HMR (a human readable *HeKatE Meta Representation*) format, and can be executed and debugged.

HeKatE provides support for the entire design process. Thanks to XTT2 rules, which are formalized with the use of the ALSV(FD) (*Attributive Logic with Set Values over Finite Domains*) [12] logic, the design process is supported with the textual HMR interpretation. XTT2 is also used to model, represent, and store the business logic of the designed systems. The process of XTT2 designing is supported by a dedicated tool, HQEd [7]. An example of XTT2 diagram is shown in Fig. 3.

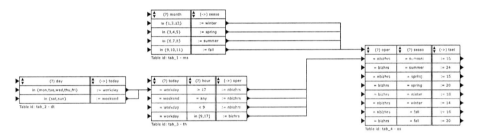

Figure 3. An example of XTT2 [12].

4.2. Drools

Drools [3], run by the JBoss Community, is a rule engine which offers knowledge integration mechanisms. Although it is not a standardized solution, the tool is well-known in the field of RBS. It is divided into four subprojects (Guvnor, Expert, Flow and Fusion), each of them supporting different parts of the integration process.

The Drools knowledge base consists of three main elements: rules, decision tables and Drools Flow. Rules, stored in text files and loaded into the program memory by dedicated Java classes, have a form of name-value pairs; they describe such parameters as rule priority and provide meta information for inference engine. Moreover, rules within the same schema can be combined into *decision tables*.

The essential part is Expert, which contains the rule engine. It collects facts from the environment, loads the knowledge base, prepares the agenda and executes rules. The inference uses a modified version of the Rete [1] algorithm. Although the decision tables are useful during the design phase, their structure does not improve the performance of the inference. They are, in fact, transformed into a flat structure of rules and the inference engine does not recognize their sources. Therefore, when the inference engine matches rules against facts, it takes all rules into consideration.

The inference process flow can be defined in Drools Flow, which offers a workflow design functionality in the form of blocks (See Fig. 4).

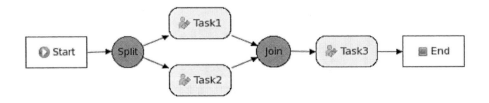

Figure 4. A sample Drools Flow diagram (see `drools.org`).

Each model in Drools Flow contains two blocks: *start* and *end*. Rules and rule flow are linked together inside the *ruleset* block. Additionally, the process can be split and joined.

As the knowledge structure represented by Drools is similar to the one represented by XTT2, an integrated approach has been proposed in [9]. Both solutions can be used to model business processes, especially in case of Drools 5, which provides some BPMN blocks.

5.   Business Processes and Business Rules Integration

A BPMN model [14] defines a BP (*Business Process*), which is a collection of related, structured tasks that produce a specific service or product (serve a particular goal) for a particular customer to accomplish the intended objectives of an organization.

According to the specification [14], BPMN is not suitable for modeling concepts, such as rules. This is due to huge differences in abstraction levels between them. However, rules can be complementary to a BP [13]. Specification of a BP can be associated with particular BRs (*Business Rules*), which define or constrain some business aspects and are intended to assert business structure or to control or influence the business behavior [6]. An example from the classic UServ Financial Services case study [2], which presents how business processes and rules can be linked, is shown in Fig. 5.

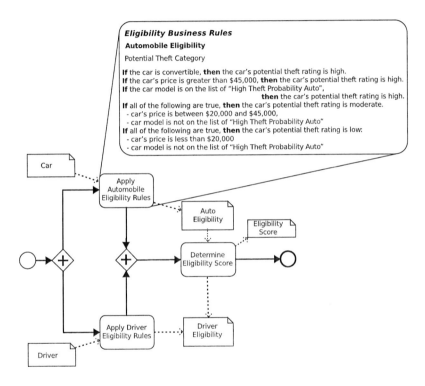

Figure 5. An example of using BR to define a process in Business Process Diagram [2].

A BPMN model has well-defined semantics and every particular model should be clear to understand. Such a model can often be simulated using particular tools, or serialized to XML and processed in BPEL4WS tools. However, execution of processes requires additional specification, which is not necessarily integrated with the entire design process. Although there are more than 70 different implementations of BPMN tools (according to OMG), no coherent proposal for BP and BR integration exists.

5.1. Integration Possibilities

The integration of BPs, described using BPMN, and BRs faces two main challenges:

Different goals: BPMN only provides a notation for modeling business processes, which define the order of tasks to accomplish the intended objectives of an organization. Although the task descriptions can be fairly detailed, it is not a proper use of the BPMN notation.

Rules, in turn, can provide a detailed and formalized description of the process logic. Moreover, there are tools which support a well-founded, systematic and complete design process [12].

Different semantics: The semantics of both solutions are different as well. BPMN describes processes, while RBS-based methods, such as XTT2, provide the description of rules. Although the semantics of each BPMN element is defined, the implementation of some particular tasks is not specified in pure BPMN. In XTT2, rules are formalized and automatic verification and execution is provided. Therefore, BPMN and RBS operate on different abstraction levels.

Several integration scenarios for XTT2 and BPMN are considered in [9]:

- **BPMN as a replacement for ARD+**
  is a scenario in which BPMN is proposed to be used instead of the HeKatE present solution – ARD+. This assumes that mapping between BPMN tasks and XTT2 tables is one-to-one. A prototype example of this approach is shown in Fig. 6 (compare to Fig. 3).

- **BPMN representation of XTT2 tables**
  is another scenario in which BPMN is proposed to be used to model XTT2, including single tables and rules. An example of this approach, the BPMN representation of *Season determining* table, can be seen in Fig. 7.

- **BPMN integration with XTT2**
  assumes that BPMN and XTT2 have some intersecting parts, in which the integration of the two solutions can be performed. In this approach, BPMN is responsible for inference specification and hierarchization of the rulebase, and rule tables for some part of the system are designed using XTT2.

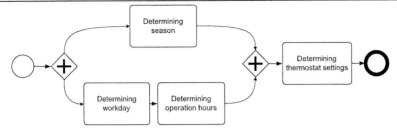

Figure 6. An example of using BPMN instead of ARD+ [9].

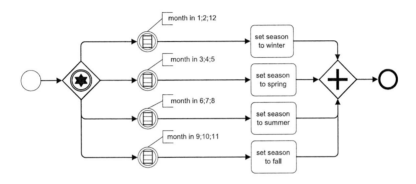

Figure 7. BPMN representation of XTT2 table [9].

The first two scenarios are rather simple. In the first one, each task is mapped to exactly one table. However, this solution does not provide the table schema, as it was in the case of ARD+. The second scenario is rather an academic one, because tables are already an efficient method of presenting rules, and their visual representation in another form may not be so useful.

The last scenario is the most complex one. It assumes that some simple tasks can be modeled in BPMN; however process logic should be modeled in XTT2. In this approach, BPMN is mainly responsible for inference specification and hierarchization of the rulebase, and rule tables for some part of the system are designed in XTT2, but the assumed mapping between tables and tasks may not be one-to-one. This should be the best scenario for real-world cases.

An example for the third scenario is a Credit Card case study. In this scenario a process of an application for a credit card is described. Fig. 8 presents a general model of a bank credit card application. When a customer sends a completed application to the bank, the credit card release procedure is started.

At the beginning, the application form is received and registered by the system. Then, a credit rating calculation takes place to determine the possible credit card limit. The next stage of the process is verification using various databases. Positive verification means that the credit card type should be determined and the message about the granted credit card should be sent to the customer. If the customer has low credit rating or the verification is negative, the customer should receive refusal information.

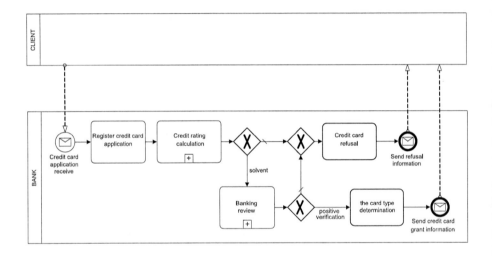

Figure 8. BPMN model of the credit card application process.

The model, shown in Fig. 8, contains two subprocesses:

- **Banking review** – the subprocess is presented in Fig. 9. Banking review consists of a number of independent verification:

  - National Debt Register BIG SA (KRD),

  - Register of European Financial Information BIG SA (ERIF),

  - Infomonitor, which is the database consists of Debtors Register of the Economic Information Bureau, Credit Information Bureau (BIK) and Polish Banks Association (PBA).

and then determining the overall verification score.

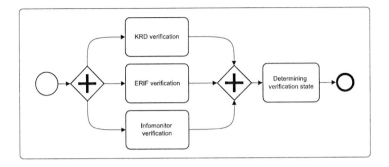

Figure 9. Banking review subprocess.

In this case, each verification score is positive or negative. Therefore, a single rule, a conjunction of all the verification scores, determines the final status of customer verification.

The Banking Law does not provide a precise description of a specific algorithm to calculate the credit rating. Thus, each bank has its own procedures for evaluating the customer credit ability. A Bank may take into account various aspects, such as the savings, insurance, account and card limits, age, occupation, etc.

- **Credit rating calculation** – the subprocess is shown in Fig. 10.

  The procedure for calculating the customer credit rating is usually comprised of a large number of rules which are dependent on specific, well-defined contexts. Thus, this process could be successfully automated by introducing RBS.

  Calculation is performed separately for each client group. Then, the highest possible credit limit is set. Tables 3 – 7 show the decision tables used to calculate the customer credit rating for each group: deposit holder, student, retired person, worker and company owner.

In the credit card application process, the last rule-based task is to determine the card type (as defined in Table 8).

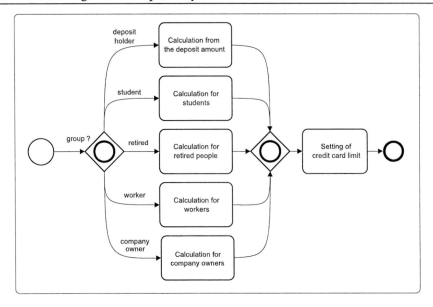

Figure 10. Credit rating calculation subprocess.

Table 3. Credit rating decision table for the *Calculation from the deposit amount* task

deposit amount ($)	deposit time (mth)	limit ($)
= any	< 12	:= 0
>= 1000	>= 12	:= mul(deposit amount,0.8)

6.   Conclusion

Practical modeling and execution of business processes is a demanding task. This chapter discusses a solution based on the use of business rules. Rules can be used both as a supportive modeling method, as well as an execution mechanism.

Practical execution of BPMs modeled with BPMN is a challenging task. To provide the background for this, selected analysis and execution methods for Business Processes, such as BPEL, and several BPMN tools have been pre-

Table 4. Credit rating decision table for the *Calculation for students* task

university	average grade	year of studies	limit ($)
= any	< 4.0	= any	:= 0
public	>= 5.0	> 1	:= 1500
public	>= 4.5	> 1	:= 1000
= any	>= 4.0	> 1	:= 500

Table 5. Credit rating decision table for the *Calculation for retired people* task

pension ($)	from (mth)	age	limit ($)
= any	= any	>= 75	:= 0
= any	< 12	= any	:= 0
< 1000	>= 12	< 75	:= 500
>= 1000	>= 12	< 75	:= mul(pension,0.8)

Table 6. Credit rating decision table for the *Calculation for workers* task

contract form	contract from (mth)	contract to (mth)	salary	limit ($)
= any	< 3	= any	= any	:= 0
= any	= any	< 12	= any	:= 0
= employment	>= 3	>= 12	< 1500	:= 500
= employment	>= 3	>= 12	>= 1500	:= mul(salary,4)
= for work	>= 6	>= 12	< 1500	:= 500
= for work	>= 6	>= 12	>= 1500	:= mul(salary,4)

sented. Since specification for software is usually vague, collaboration between business analysts and SOA architects is necessary at all software development stages. Advanced commercial tools support such collaboration by employing one of the two approaches to integrity assurance, as defined in Section 3.3. Commercial solutions presented in the comparison implement a set of func-

Table 7. Credit rating decision table for the *Calculation for company owners* task

average income (6 mth in $)	company from (years)	limit ($)
= any	< 1	:= 0
< 2000	>= 1	:= 500
>= 2000	[1;2]	:= average income
>= 2000	> 2	:= mul(average income,4)

Table 8. Decision table for the *Card type determining* task

limit ($)	card type
[500;2000)	:= amber
[2000;10000)	:= silver
[10000;40000)	:= gold
> 40000	:= platinum

tions necessary to deploy SOA in an enterprise, but they may not provide the necessary flexibility. Therefore, due to the smaller feature set of *open source* tools, they may be a better starting point for extension and implementation of more advanced and non-standard functionalities.

An important issue is the quality assurance of BPMs. This often requires verification procedures. Since there are well-established methods for verification and optimization in the RBS area, the solution presented in this chapter uses a rule-based methodology. In Section 4., selected Rule-Based solutions, such as Drools and XTT2 – a novel visual rule specification that provides formalized analysis – have been described. BPs can be supported with BRs as the executable logic. In the chapter, integration of XTT2 with BPMN has been considered. In this case, the BPMN model specifies a behavior while rules provide a description of low-level logic.

References

[1] Szymon Bobek, Krzysztof Kaczor, and Grzegorz J. Nalepa. Overview of rule inference algorithms for structured rule bases. *Gdansk University of Technology Faculty of ETI Annals*, 18(8):57–62, 2010.

[2] BRForum. UServ Product Derby case study. Technical report, Business Rules Forum, 2005.

[3] Paul Browne. *JBoss Drools Business Rules*. Packt Publishing, 2009.

[4] Thomas Erl. *Service-Oriented Architecture (SOA): Concepts, Technology, and Design*. Prentice Hall PTR, 2005.

[5] Yi Gao. BPMN – BPEL transformation and round trip engineering. Technical report, eClarus Software, 2006.

[6] D. Hay, A. Kolber, and K. Anderson Healy. Defining Business Rules – what they really are. final report. Technical report, Business Rules Group, July 2000.

[7] Krzysztof Kaczor and Grzegorz J. Nalepa. Extensible design and verification enviroment for XTT rule bases. In *CMS'09: Computer Methods and Systems: 7th conference, 26–27 November 2009, Kraków, Poland*. AGH University of Science and Technology, Cracow, Oprogramowanie Naukowo-Techniczne, 2009.

[8] Krzysztof Kluza and Grzegorz J. Nalepa. MOF-based metamodeling for the XTT knowledge representation. In *CMS'09: Computer Methods and Systems: 7th conference, 26–27 November 2009, Kraków, Poland*. AGH University of Science and Technology, Cracow, Oprogramowanie Naukowo-Techniczne, 2009.

[9] Krzysztof Kluza, Grzegorz J. Nalepa, and Łukasz Łysik. Visual inference specification methods for modularized rulebases. Overview and integration proposal. In Grzegorz J. Nalepa and Joachim Baumeister, editors, *6th Workshop on Knowledge Engineering and Software Engineering (KESE2009) at the 32nd German conference on Artificial Intelligence: September 21, 2010, Karlsruhe, Germany*, pages 6–17, Karlsruhe, Germany, 2010.

[10] Antoni Ligęza. *Logical Foundations for Rule-Based Systems*. Springer-Verlag, Berlin, Heidelberg, 2006.

[11] Antoni Ligęza and Grzegorz J. Nalepa. Rules verification and validation. In Kuldar Taveter Adrian Giurca, Dragan Gasevic, editor, *Handbook of Research on Emerging Rule-Based Languages and Technologies: Open Solutions and Approaches*, pages 273–301. IGI Global, Hershey, New York, 2009.

[12] Grzegorz J. Nalepa and Antoni Ligęza. HeKatE methodology, hybrid engineering of intelligent systems. *International Journal of Applied Mathematics and Computer Science*, 20(1):35–53, March 2010.

[13] Grzegorz J. Nalepa and Maria A. Mach. Business Rules design method for Business Process Management. In M. Ganzha and M. Paprzycki, editors, *Proceedings of the International Multiconference on Computer Science and Information Technology*, pages 165–170. Polish Information Processing Society, IEEE Computer Society Press, 2009.

[14] OMG. Business Process Modeling Notation (BPMN) specification. Technical Report dtc/06-02-01, Object Management Group, February 2006.

[15] Kapil Pant and Matjaz Juric. *Business Process Driven SOA using BPMN and BPEL: From Business Process Modeling to Orchestration and Service Oriented Architecture*. Packt Publishing, 2008.

[16] A. I. Vermesan and F. Coenen, editors. *Validation and Verification of Knowledge Based Systems. Theory, Tools and Practice*. Kluwer Academic Publisher, Boston, 1999.

[17] Maciej Zakrzewicz. Tutorial: Implementacja aplikacji biznesowych w technologii WS-BPEL. Technical report, PLOUG, 2006.

In: Business Process Modeling
Editor: Jason A. Beckmann

ISBN: 978-1-61209-344-4
© 2011 Nova Science Publishers, Inc.

Chapter 7

Optimal Capacity Planning and Performance Evaluation in a Process-Based Business with the Consideration of System Failures

Shin-Guang Chen*
Department of Industrial Engineering and Management
Tungnan University, Taipei County 222, Taiwan

Abstract

Business process modeling is an important stage in Business Process
Management (BPM). There are many tools and methodologies to do such
modeling. However, few of them can provide an optimal planning as well
as the performance evaluation in a versatile environment. Since the globalized economics changes very fast, the process dynamic state for each
firm also changes day by day. Our approach can provide companies a
helpful toolkit to manage such situation while keeping the ability to predict the performance of each business process. Due to IT advances in Enterprise Resource Planning Systems (ERPS), more and more companies
adapted Service-Oriented Architecture (SOA) as the main infrastructure
of their core business operations. So, process is the key identity of business activity to be monitored. However, how to capacitate (man or machine) as well as to evaluate the performance of such process, especially

*E-mail address: bobchen@mail.tnu.edu.tw

in a volatile environment, so that the business goal can be fulfilled is still unknown to most of the mangers. This chapter proposes an integrated method to do both optimal capacity planning and performance evaluation for the companies facing people floating as well as system failures while keeping the capability to predict the performance of such process. So, the planning decision can be verified. A numerical example is illustrated for the proposed method.

PACS 05.45-a, 52.35.Mw, 96.50.Fm.

Keywords: Capacity planning, performance evaluation, staff planning, optimization, system failure, process network, minimal path.

AMS Subject Classification: 53D, 37C, 65P.

1. Introduction

Due to IT advances in Enterprise Resource Planning Systems (ERPS), more and more companies adapted Service-Oriented Architecture (SOA) as the main infrastructure of their core business operations across nations. SOA was known to achieve agility, efficiency and flexibility of core processes in companies (Lawler et al., 2009). So, process is the key identity of business activity which can be monitored. Nowadays, IT technologies allow the operation in a process be completed either by persons or by machines. The capacity planning here includes the planning of persons as well as machines in the underlined process. The normal Human Resource Management (HRM) practices may not be well-fitted for such a process-based staffing, because they are based on a static environment (Armstrong, 2006). Anderson Jr. (2007) proposed an elegant staffing method based on random walk for a nonstationary environment, but his approach only applied for the solution of a long-term business cycle. For a short-term operation, this may not be appropriate. Eveborn and Ronnqvist (2004) introduced a program, Scheduler, which can give a staff schedule based on the short-term static data, but they did not create the number of persons a process optimally required. For machine planning aspect, Perrone et al. (2002) presented a long-term capacity decision in uncertain markets by scope economics. Their model could not answer the question of detailed plans for an Automated System (AS). Arbel and Seidmann (1984) proposed a performance evaluation method for Flexible System (FS) based on Analytic Hierarchy Process (AHP) heuristics. Such approach can only obtain a consistent subjective evaluation. A similar AHP-based approach was presented by Nagalingam and Lin (1998). When an AS is given , the capacity planning problem becomes the scheduling problem for machines (Crama, 1997). For example, Bilgin and Azizoglu (2009) proposed the Tabu heuristics to search for a near optimal capacity allocation plan for an AS, but they did not provide the performance verification of such plan. Hence, how to plan as well as to evaluate the performance of such process, especially in a volatile environment, so that the business goal can be fulfilled is still unknown to most of the mangers. Chen and Lin (2008b) first proposed an analytic method to evaluate the Bayesian performance of a business process. Later, they further introduced a method to give the linguistic performance for a business process (Chen and Lin, 2009). Chen (2009) extended it to cover the performance of a business process in case of system failures. Chen and Lin's model gave the excellent solution to evaluate the short-term performance for a process even in a volatile environment.

In this chapter, we base on the Chen and Lin's approach (Chen and Lin, 2008a) to generate an optimal capacity plan in a process-based business under both absentees and machine failures such that the required total cost for process is minimal and the performance of the process is acceptable. So, the approach not only narrows the whole search space and searches for the optimal plan, but also calculates the derived performance simultaneously. A process network is defined as that the nodes of the net are the persons or machines responsible for the operations of the processes. The arcs are the precedence relationships (or the systems) between processes. So, the node or arc have multi-states or -capacity and may fail (i.e., having absentees, machine or system failures). The faults in such a network usually depict a decrease in capacity of the component (node or arc) and that stops the network due to an insufficient supply of document flow (i.e., the low performance). A conventional way to work out such issues is to increase the number of persons or machines for each operation respectively. That is, for demand d, a trivial plan is to let the maximal capacity of each component equal d. Such a scheme is not optimal and considered less benefit in cost. This chapter proposes an algorithm to narrow down the whole search space, which is based on the structural analysis for the network and further assessed by the critical analysis. The structural analysis is to identify the structurally important components which can not fail during the system operation. The critical analysis identifies the critical components of the underlined network. A component is critical if and only if its failure causes the system performance dropped to zero. Thus, a network full of critical components is very fragile. Any component's failure may stop the functionality of the process immediately. So, a network is robust if and only if any failure in non-critical components would not stop the net work. In this chapter, the calculation of system performance is based on Minimal Path (MP) (Chen and Lin, 2008b; Hudson and Kapur, 1983; Jane and Laih, 2008; Lin, 2001; Yeh, 2005). An MP is a sequence of nodes and arcs from source to sink without cycles. This chapter addresses the optimal conditions for such a network and illustrates the efficiency of the proposed algorithm by a numerical example. The remainder of the work is described as follows: The mathematical preliminaries and assumptions for the approach is presented in Section 2. Section 3 describes the theories for optimal capacity planning. Section 4 describes the algorithm of searching for such optimal plan. Then, the proposed method is illustrated by a numerical example in Section 5. Section 6 concludes this chapter.

2. Preliminaries

Let $G = (V,E,M,C,W)$ be a process network where $E = \{a_i | 1 \leq i \leq n\}$ is the set of arcs, $V = \{a_i | n+1 \leq i \leq n+s\}$ is the set of nodes, and $M = (m_1, m_2, \ldots, m_{n+s})$ is a vector with m_i (an integer) being the maximal capacity of component a_i (nodes or arcs). M is normally allocated by experience and strongly affects the cost. It is treated as a constant vector here, however, it will be treated as a variable vector later to be solved in this chapter. $C = (c_1, c_2, \ldots, c_{n+s})$ is the cost vector for components. W is the penalty when process failed. Such a G is assumed to satisfy the following assumptions.

1. The capacity of each component a_i is an integer-valued random variable which takes values from the set $\{0,1,2,\ldots,m_i\}$ according to a given distribution. Note that 0 often denotes a failure or being unavailable.

2. The persons or machines in the same operation of the process have the same work capability and the same availability respectively.

3. Flow in G must satisfy the flow-conservation law (Ford and Fulkerson, 1962).

4. The components are statistically independent from each other.

2.1. The Process Network Model

Suppose mp_1, mp_2, ..., mp_z are totally the MPs from the source to the sink. Thus, the network model can be described in terms of two vectors: the capacity vector $X = (x_1, x_2, \ldots, x_{n+s})$ and the flow vector $F = (f_1, f_2, \ldots, f_z)$ where x_i denotes the current capacity on a_i and f_j denotes the current flow on mp_j. Then such a vector F is feasible if and only if

$$\sum_{j=1}^{z} \{f_j | a_i \in mp_j\} \leq m_i \quad \text{for each } i = 1, 2, \ldots, n+s. \tag{1}$$

Equation (1) describes that the total flow through a_i can not exceed the maximal capacity on a_i. We denote such set of F as $U_M \equiv \{F | F \text{ is feasible under } M\}$. Similarly, F is feasible under $X = (x_1, x_2, \ldots, x_{n+s})$ if and only if

$$\sum_{j=1}^{z} \{f_j | a_i \in mp_j\} \leq x_i \quad \text{for each } i = 1, 2, \ldots, n+s. \tag{2}$$

For clarity, let $U_X = \{F | F \text{ is feasible under } X\}$. The maximal flow under X is defined as $MV(X) \equiv \max\{\sum_{j=1}^{z} f_j | F \in U_X\}$.

2.2. System Performance Evaluation

Given a demand d, the system performance R_d is the probability that the maximal flow is no less than d, i.e., $R_d \equiv \Pr\{X | MV(X) \geq d\}$. To calculate R_d, it is advantageously to find the minimal vector in the set $\{X | MV(X) \geq d\}$. A minimal vector X is said to be a lower boundary point (LBP) for d if and only if (i) $MV(X) \geq d$ and (ii) $MV(Y) < d$ for any other vector Y such that $Y < X$, in which $Y \leq X$ if and only if $y_j \leq x_j$ for each $j = 1, 2, \ldots, n+s$ and $Y < X$ if and only if $Y \leq X$ and $y_j < x_j$ for at least one j. Suppose there are totally t LBPs for d, $X_1, X_2, \ldots, X_t$. The system performance is equal to

$$R_d = \Pr\{\bigcup_{k=1}^{t} \{X | X \geq X_k\}\}. \tag{3}$$

2.3. Probability Calculation Scheme

To calculate Equation (3), the probability for $\Pr\{X_i\}$ of component a_i should be defined in advance. This can be done by assuming that there are e_i persons or machines for component a_i to produce the corresponding capacity. Each person or machine has the availability of r_i. Then the probability for the current capacity X_i is denoted as a binomial distribution:

$$\Pr\{X_i = k\} = \binom{e_i}{k} r_i^k (1 - r_i)^{e_i - k}. \tag{4}$$

2.4. Generation of All LBPs for d

At first, we find the flow vector $F \in U_M$ such that the total flow of F equals d. It is defined in the following demand constraint,

$$\sum_{j=1}^{z} f_j = d. \tag{5}$$

Then, let $\mathbf{F}=\{F | F \in U_M$ and satisfies Equation (5)$\}$. We show that if an LBP X for d exists then there is an $F \in \mathbf{F}$ by the following lemmas.

Lemma 2.1. *If X is an LBP for d, then there is an $F \in \mathbf{F}$ such that*

$$x_i = \sum_{j=1}^{z} \{f_j | a_i \in mp_j\} \quad \text{for each } i = 1, 2, \ldots, n+s. \tag{6}$$

Proof. If X is a lower boundary point for d, then there is an F such that $F \in U_X$ and $F \in \mathbf{F}$. It is known that $\sum_{j=1}^{z} \{f_j | a_i \in mp_j\} \le x_i \ \forall i$. Suppose there is a k such that $x_k > \sum_{j=1}^{z} \{f_j | a_k \in mp_j\}$. Set $Y = (y_1, y_2, \ldots, y_{k-1}, y_k, y_{k+1}, \ldots, y_{n+s}) = (x_1, x_2, \ldots, x_{k-1}, x_k - 1, x_{k+1}, \ldots, x_{n+s})$. Hence $Y < X$ and $F \in U_Y$ (since $\sum_{j=1}^{z} \{f_j | a_i \in mp_j\} \le y_i \ \forall i$), which indicates that $MV(Y) \ge d$ and contradicts to that X is a lower boundary point for d. Thus $x_i = \sum_{j=1}^{z} \{f_j | a_i \in mp_j\} \ \forall i$. □

Given $F \in \mathbf{F}$, we generate a capacity vector $X_F = (x_1, x_2, \ldots, x_{n+s})$ via Equation (6). Then the set $\Omega = \{X_F | F \in \mathbf{F}\}$ is built. Let $\Omega_{min} = \{X | X$ is a minimal vector in $\Omega\}$. Lemma 2.1 implies that the set Ω includes all LBPs for d. The following lemma further proves that Ω_{min} is the set of LBPs for d.

Lemma 2.2. Ω_{min} *is the set of LBPs for d.*

Proof. Firstly, suppose $X \in \Omega_{min}$ (note that $MV(X) \geq d$) but it is not a lower boundary point for d. Then, there is a lower boundary point Y for d such that $Y < X$, which implies $Y \in \Omega$ and thus contradicts to that $X \in \Omega_{min}$. Hence X is a lower boundary point for d. Conversely, suppose X is a lower boundary point for d (note that $X \in \Omega$) but $X \notin \Omega_{min}$ i.e., there is a $Y \in \Omega$ such that $Y < X$. Then $MV(Y) \geq d$ which contradicts to that X is a lower boundary point for d. Hence $X \in \Omega_{min}$. □

3. Capacity Planning

Our problem is to find a proper M such that the network is survived and the required total cost is minimal and the performance can be derived. We develop theories to show how to narrow down the search space for this problem. Given a network, the MPs are determined by the topology of the network. One can analyze the flow of a component via the binding MPs. Let $P_i = \{mp_j | a_i \in mp_j\}$ denote the subset of MPs binding with a_i. We define the coverage set Q_i of a_i by the following definition.

Definition 3.1. (Coverage set): *Let $a_i, a_j \in V$. a_j is covered by a_i if and only if $P_j \subseteq P_i$, and $j \in Q_i$.*

Definition 3.1 implies that there is no flow through a_j if a_i totally failed. A structural impact (SI) S_i for a_i is then defined as:

Definition 3.2. (SI): $S_i = \frac{||\{a_j | P_j \subseteq P_i\}||}{n+s}$.

The symbol $|| \bullet ||$ denotes the total number of elements in the set. "$n+s$" is the total number of components in the network. If $S_i = 1.0$, it means that a_i covers all components in the network and has the strongest structural impact upon the network. The smaller S_i is, the less impact a_i has. S_i can not be zero, since it must cover itself.

3.1. Critical Analysis

If the capacity of a component is decreased to zero (i.e., totally failed) while keeping the other components unchanged, we can analyze the derived impact of the network via performance. The calculated performance is thought as a "survivability" for d of the network when the specific component totally failed. It is defined as:

Definition 3.3. (Survivability): $R_{d,i}$ *is the derived performance when a_i totally failed.*

This concept can be extended to the identification of critical components.

Definition 3.4. (Critical component): *a_i is critical if and only if $R_{d,i} = 0$.*

From Definition 3.4 and 3.2, we have the following lemma.

Lemma 3.1. *a_i is critical if $S_i = 1.0$.*

Proof. By definition. □

This implies that a_i may be non-critical if $S_i < 1.0$.

3.2. Robustness

Given M, a network G is robust if it satisfied the following definition:

Definition 3.5. (Robustness): *M is robust for d if and only if $R_{d,i} > 0$ for all i such that $S_i < 1.0$.*

That is, if a vector M is robust for d, it should provide sufficient capacity to support such failure except those are structurally important. It can be shown that $m_i \geq d \ \forall i$ is a sufficient condition for M to be robust.

Lemma 3.2. *M is robust for d if $m_i \geq d \ \forall i$.*

Proof. Suppose $m_i \geq d \ \forall i$. There are a_j and a_k, $j \neq k$, such that $R_{d,j} = 0$. $R_{d,j} = 0$ means that the total flow of the network is insufficient for demand d. This implies that $\sum_{l=1}^{z}\{f_l | a_k \in mp_l\} \leq m_k < \sum_{l=1}^{z} f_l < d$, which contradicts to that $m_k \geq d$. So $R_{d,j} > 0$. M is robust for d. □

However, when M is robust, it is not necessary for all m_i to be greater than d. The combination of flows may fulfill the demand d. Lemma 3.2 only describes the fact that d is a feasible upper bound for m_i. Our goal is then restated as to find a feasible lower bound of m_i to support robustness for d such that the total cost is minimal and the performance is predictable. A novel way is to inspect the capacity vector in LBPs generated by initially setting all $m_i = d$. By

Equations (5) and (6), an LBP is a minimal capacity vector such that the total flow in G equals d. Lemma 3.2 shows that the set of LBPs when initially setting all $m_i = d$ can not be empty. Although an LBP is generated after given M, the column value in the vector is less than or equal to the corresponding m_i. If we reduce m_i of each component to the corresponding column value of LBP, G still survived for d. However, no capacity of any column can be further de creased, since an LBP is a minimal vector to support G being survived for d. Similarly, if G is robust when a_i failed, a feasible vector for the remaining components can be derived from the LBPs generated by $G \backslash \{a_i\}$. The newly derived capacity can cover the lost flow of a_i. Let $\Phi = \{i \, | S_i < 1.0\}$ be the index set of the structurally unimportant components, and $\Omega_{min,i}$ denote the set of LBPs generated after setting $m_i = 0$ and $m_j = d$ for any $j \neq i$. The LBPs generated from $\Omega_{min,i}$ can be used as a guide to select the minimal M. However, an LBP may consist of numerous zeros in the vector, which are undesired for applications (i.e., they are corresponding to the faulty components). Consequently, a vector with the least zeros is preferable for choice. To filter out the LBPs with undesired zeros, an efficient strategy based on SI value can be applied. We firstly show that if the flow of the self-covering component a_i (i.e., $S_i = 1/(n+s)$) is greater than 0, then the flow of other components covering a_i would not be zero. That is, the flow of such a_i will dominate the non-zero flow to other components.

Lemma 3.3. *For a_i with $S_i = 1/(n+s)$, if $\sum_{k=1}^{z}\{f_k|a_i \in mp_k\} > 0$, then*

$$\sum_{k=1}^{z}\{f_k|a_j \in mp_k\} > 0 \quad \forall a_j \text{ covering } a_i, \, j \neq i. \tag{7}$$

Proof. Since a_j covers a_i, then $\sum_{k=1}^{z}\{f_k|a_j \in mp_k\} \geq \sum_{k=1}^{z}\{f_k|a_i \in mp_k\} > 0$. It holds. $\qquad\square$

In some cases, we may have $||P_i|| = 1$ but $S_i > 1/(n+s)$ for a_i. This indicates that a_i is serially concatenated with some other components. Such group of components are treated as one self-covering component. We only take into account the first occurrence of component in the same MP. Let $\varphi = \{i \, | S_i = 1/(n+s)$ or the first a_i in the same MP such that $||P_i|| = 1\}$ be the index set of the self-covering components.

Then, we can inspect those columns corresponding to the self-covering components in each LBP generated from $\Omega_{min,i}$. There are two conditions for inspection. One is $||\varphi \backslash Q_i|| \leq d$, and the other is $||\varphi \backslash Q_i|| > d$. The former denotes the supply of flow d is sufficient for all self-covering components and so are the other components. If any self-covering component is not zero, then every other component should cover at least one self-covering component and its flow would not be zero. In this case, one can directly delete those LBPs generated from $\Omega_{min,i}$ with zero columns other than column i and its coverage columns (which should be zero). The latter condition states the insufficient flow situation. In this case, one even dispatch flow d to each self-covering component by only 1 unit of flow, there are still some other self-covering components with zero flow. However, such vector consists of the least number of zeros among all other LBPs. That is, one can delete those LBPs with columns corresponding to the self-covering components having the value greater than 1. Such filtering process can keep the vectors with the least number of zeros in hand and decrease the search space tremendously for M. It can be shown that the filtered $\Omega_{min,i}$ has the possible range of lower bound for M. Let $X = (x_1, x_2, \ldots, x_{n+s})$ be an LBP in $\Omega_{min,i}$, then

Theorem 3.1. $M = (m_1, m_2, \ldots, m_{n+s})$ is robust for d if and only if

$$m_j = \max\{x_j | X \in \Omega_{min,i} \, \forall i \in \Phi\} \text{ for } j = 1, 2, \ldots, n+s. \qquad (8)$$

Proof. Suppose M is robust for d, then $R_{d,i} > 0$ for all i in Φ. We can find m_j such that $x_j = \sum_{k=1}^{z}\{f_k | a_j \in mp_k\} \leq m_j$ for $j = 1, 2, \ldots, n+s$, $\forall i \in \Phi$. So m_j is a maximum. Conversely, let $m_j = \max\{x_j | X \in \Omega_{min,i} \, \forall i \in \Phi\}$ for $j = 1, 2, \ldots, n+s$. Then, $m_j \geq x_j = \sum_{k=1}^{z}\{f_k | a_j \in mp_k\} \, \forall j$. This implies $R_{d,i} > 0$. Then, M is robust for d. $\square$

Theorem 3.1 shows that such M exists. We denote such set as $\Gamma \equiv \{M | M$ is robust for $d\}$. The performance under M is defined as $R_d(M)$. The optimal capacity plan for M would be the solution for the following non-linear integer programming problem:

$$Minimize \quad \sum_{j=1}^{n+s} m_j c_j + Wd(1 - R_d(M)) \quad subject \ to \ M \in \Gamma. \qquad (9)$$

Let $M_{i,j} = \{x_j | x_j > 0 \, \forall X \in \Omega_{min,i}\}$ denote the set of possible values for column j. We further define $M_{min,j} = \max\{x_j | x_j \in M_{i,j}$ and x_j is minimal $\forall i \in \Phi\}$ as the largest minimal value among i for column j and $M_{max,j} = \max\{x_j | x_j \in M_{i,j}$ and x_j is maximal $\forall i \in \Phi\}$ as the largest maximal value among i for column j. One can show that for any $M \in \Gamma$, m_j exists in the interval $[M_{min,j}, M_{max,j}]$.

Theorem 3.2. *If* $M = (m_1, m_2, \ldots, m_{n+s}) \in \Gamma$, *then*

$$M_{min,j} \leq m_j \leq M_{max,j} \quad \text{for } j = 1, 2, \ldots, n+s.$$

Proof. From Theorem 3.1, if $m_j = \max\{x_j | X \in \Omega_{min,i} \; \forall i \in \Phi\}$, then $\max\{x_j | X \in \Omega_{min,i} \; \forall i \in \Phi\} \geq \max\{x_j | x_j \in M_{i,j} \text{ and } x_j \text{ is minimal } \forall i \in \Phi\} = M_{min,j}$. So, $m_j \geq M_{min,j}$. Similarly, $\max\{x_j | X \in \Omega_{min,i} \; \forall i \in \Phi\} \leq \max\{x_j | x_j \in M_{i,j} \text{ and } x_j \text{ is maximal } \forall i \in \Phi\} = M_{max,j}$, then $m_j \leq M_{max,j}$. It holds. ☐

For clarity, we define $\mathbf{m}_j = \{m_j | M_{min,j} \leq m_j \leq M_{max,j}\}$ as the interval set for column j. One can show that $\Gamma \subseteq \mathbf{m}_1 \times \mathbf{m}_2 \times \ldots \times \mathbf{m}_{n+s}$, where the symbol "$\times$" denotes the Cartesian product among sets and is defined as $\mathbf{m}_1 \times \mathbf{m}_2 = \{(x,y) | x \in \mathbf{m}_1 \text{ and } y \in \mathbf{m}_2\}$.

Theorem 3.3. $\Gamma \subseteq \mathbf{m}_1 \times \mathbf{m}_2 \times \ldots \times \mathbf{m}_{n+s}$.

Proof. By Theorem 3.2. ☐

Theorem 3.3 denotes that the set $\mathbf{m}_1 \times \mathbf{m}_2 \times \ldots \times \mathbf{m}_{n+s}$ includes all the feasible M in Γ. This implies that Γ can be searched from the much smaller Cartesian product.

4. Algorithm

Let $\Omega_i = \{X_F | F \in \mathbf{F} \text{ under } m_i = 0\}$. The following algorithm is proposed to find the optimal M for d.

Algorithm 1: The optimal capacity plan of process G for d.

1. For $i \in \Phi$ do // for structurally unimportant components.

   (a) Initially set $m_i = 0$, $m_k = d$ for any $k \neq i$. Generates $\Omega_{min,i}$ as in the following:

   i. Compute $\mathbf{F}$ for satisfying $\sum_{k=1}^{z}\{f_k | a_l \in mp_k\} \leq m_l$ and $\sum_{k=1}^{z} f_k = d$.

   ii. Construct Ω_i via X_F, which is formed by $x_l = \sum_{k=1}^{z}\{f_k | a_l \in mp_k\}$.

   iii. Generate $\Omega_{min,i}$ via simple comparison. //i.e., pairwise comparison.

(b) For $X \in \Omega_{min,i}$ do // The filtering process.

    If $||\varphi \backslash Q_i|| \leq d$, then

        For $1 \leq l \leq n+s$ do

            If $x_l = 0$ and $l \neq i$ and $l \notin Q_i$, then $\Omega_{min,i} = \Omega_{min,i} \backslash \{X\}$.

        End for.

    Else,

        For $1 \leq l \leq n+s$ do

            If $x_l > 1$ and $l \in \varphi$, then $\Omega_{min,i} = \Omega_{min,i} \backslash \{X\}$.

        End for.

    End for.

End for.

2. For $i \in \Phi$ do // Construct $M_{i,j}$

    For $X \in \Omega_{min,i}$ do

        For $1 \leq j \leq n+s$ do

            If $x_j \notin M_{i,j}$ and $x_j > 0$, then $M_{i,j} = M_{i,j} \cup \{x_j\}$.

        End for.

    End for.

End for.

3. For $1 \leq j \leq n+s$ do // Construct $\mathbf{m}_j$

    $M_{min,j} = \max\{x_j | x_j \in M_{i,j}$ and x_j is minimal, $\forall i \in \Phi\}$.

    $M_{max,j} = \max\{x_j | x_j \in M_{i,j}$ and x_j is maximal, $\forall i \in \Phi\}$.

    $\mathbf{m}_j = \{m_j | M_{min,j} \leq m_j \leq M_{max,j}\}$.

End for.

4. For $M \in \mathbf{m}_1 \times \mathbf{m}_2 \times \ldots \times \mathbf{m}_{n+s}$ do // Construct Γ.

    Set $CNT = 0$ // CNT is a counter for Φ

    For $i \in \Phi$ do

        For $X \in \Omega_{min,i}$ do

            If $M \geq X$, then $CNT = CNT + 1$ and break.

End for.

End for.

If $CNT = ||\Phi||$, then $\Gamma = \Gamma \cup \{M\}$.

End for.

5. Let $sum_C = (n+s)dW$. // $(n+s)dW$ is a feasible large number.

6. For $M \in \Gamma$ do // Search for the optimal M.

If $\sum_{j=1}^{n+s} m_j c_j + Wd(1 - R_d(M)) < sum_C$, then $M_{best} = M$ and $sum_C = \sum_{j=1}^{n+s} m_j c_j + Wd(1 - R_d(M))$.

End for.

7. Output: The optimal capacity plan is M_{best}, the lowest cost is sum_C and the performance is $R_d(M_{best})$.

For $i \in \Phi$, Step (1) generates $\Omega_{min,i}$ for d. Step (1b) filters out the vectors with undesired zeros. Step (4) constructs the candidate set Γ. Step (6) finds the best choice of M, where R_d is calculated via $\Pr\{\bigcup_{k=1}^{t}\{X|X \geq X_k\}\}$ and X_k is the LBP in Ω_{min} under M. Since the computation of R_d is not emphasized in this chapter, the following complexity will exclude the complexity derived from the computation of R_d.

4.1. Storage Complexity

The number of solutions for $\mathbf{F}$ is bounded by $\binom{z+d-1}{z-1}$. The number of X_F generated is then bounded by $\binom{z+d-1}{z-1}$. The storage space needed for all the final $\Omega_{min,i}$ (i.e., the filtered set) is then bounded by $O((n+s)\binom{z+d-1}{z-1})$ in the worst case. Let $n_i = ||\Omega_{min,i}||$, then the number of $M_{i,j}$ is bounded by $O(\sum_{i \in \Phi} d(n+s)n_i)$. The number of Γ is then bounded by $O(\binom{||\varphi||}{d} \prod_{k=1}^{n+s-||\varphi||} ||\mathbf{m}_k||)$ in the worst case. In sum, the total storage space needed is $O(\binom{||\varphi||}{d} \prod_{k=1}^{n+s-||\varphi||} ||\mathbf{m}_k||)$ in the worst case.

4.2. Computational Complexity

A pairwise comparison is required for generating $\Omega_{min,i}$ between $\binom{z+d-1}{z-1}$ solutions. This takes $O((n+s)^2 \binom{z+d-1}{z-1})$ time to generate all the final $\Omega_{min,i}$. To generate Γ, it spends $O((n+s)\prod_{i=1}^{n+s}||\mathbf{m}_i|| \sum_{k=1}^{n+s} n_k)$ time in the worst case. Then, it consumes $O(||\Gamma||)$ time to test the best M. In short, the total computational time required is $O((n+s)\prod_{i=1}^{n+s}||\mathbf{m}_i|| \sum_{k=1}^{n+s} n_k)$ in the worst case.

5. Numerical Example

Suppose a business process exists to sale goods. Two alternative factories located at Shanghai and Taipei dispatched by SAP ERP systems respectively can be employed concurrently to produce these goods. There are four machine centers (MCs) connected the first two factories by conveyors (Cs) but MC 3 is located at Shanghai and it can receive work orders from Taipei and send back goods via boat. Two delivery departments connected the four previous machine centers by trucks (Ts) or boat. Finally, the payment department closes all these orders via two Fax channels. Figure 1 denotes such process network. We want to know how many persons or machines for each operation in this network to support a demand of 400 goods per day such that the total cost is minimal and the performance is acceptable. The data for this example are listed in Table 1. There are totally 7 MPs existed: $mp_1 = \{a_{15}, a_1, a_{16}, a_3, a_{18}, a_8, a_{22}, a_{13}, a_{24}\}$, $mp_2 = \{a_{15}, a_1, a_{16}, a_4, a_{19}, a_9, a_{22}, a_{13}, a_{24}\}$, $mp_3 = \{a_{15}, a_1, a_{16}, a_5, a_{20}, a_{10}, a_{22}, a_{13}, a_{24}\}$, $mp_4 = \{a_{15}, a_1, a_{16}, a_5, a_{20}, a_{11}, a_{23}, a_{14}, a_{24}\}$, $mp_5 = \{a_{15}, a_2, a_{17}, a_6, a_{20}, a_{10}, a_{22}, a_{13}, a_{24}\}$, $mp_6 = \{a_{15}, a_2, a_{17}, a_6, a_{20}, a_{11}, a_{23}, a_{14}, a_{24}\}$, and $mp_7 = \{a_{15}, a_2, a_{17}, a_7, a_{21}, a_{12}, a_{23}, a_{14}, a_{24}\}$. Assume the historical availability and cost (normalized by capacity), the coverage set, and SI for each component are listed in Table 2. The penalty is 12 (in $\$10^3$ per capacity).

The capacity (in 10^2 goods) for each component of the process is planned according to the following steps.

1. For $i = 1$ do // $\Phi = \{1, 2, \ldots, 24\} \backslash \{15, 24\}$.

(a) Initially set $m_1 = 0$, $m_k = 4$ and $k \neq 1$. Generates $\Omega_{min,1}$ as follows:

i. Compute $\mathbf{F}$, satisfying $\sum_{k=1}^{7} \{f_k | a_l \in mp_k\} \leq m_l$ and $\sum_{k=1}^{7} f_k = 4$.

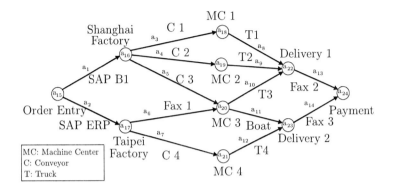

Figure 1. A order fulfillment process.

Table 1. The data for Figure 1.

Dep./Sys.	Order Entry	SAP B1	SAP ERP	Shanghai	Taipei	Delivery
Goods per day	100*	400	400	100*	100*	50*

Dep./Sys.	Boat	MC	T	C	Fax	Payment
Goods per day	400	100	100	400	50	100*

* Goods per day per person.

$\mathbf{F} = \{(0, 0, 0, 0, 0, 0, 4), (0, 0, 0, 0, 0, 1, 3), (0, 0, 0, 0, 0, 2, 2), (0, 0, 0, 0, 0, 3, 1), (0, 0, 0, 0, 0, 4, 0), (0, 0, 0, 0, 1, 0, 3), (0, 0, 0, 0, 1, 1, 2), (0, 0, 0, 0, 1, 2, 1), (0, 0, 0, 0, 1, 3, 0), (0, 0, 0, 0, 2, 0, 2), (0, 0, 0, 0, 2, 1, 1), (0, 0, 0, 0, 2, 2, 0), (0, 0, 0, 0, 3, 0, 1), (0, 0, 0, 0, 3, 1, 0), (0, 0, 0, 0, 4, 0, 0)\}.$

ii. Construct Ω_1 via X_F, which is formed by $x_l = \sum_{k=1}^{7} \{f_k | a_l \in mp_k\}$.

$\Omega_1 = \{(0, 4, 0, 0, 0, 0, 4, 0, 0, 0, 0, 4, 0, 4, 4, 0, 4, 0, 0, 0, 4, 0, 4, 4), (0, 4, 0, 0, 0, 1, 3, 0, 0, 0, 1, 3, 0, 4, 4, 0, 4, 0, 0, 1, 3, 0, 4, 4), (0, 4, 0, 0, 0, 2, 2, 0, 0, 0, 2, 2, 0, 4, 4, 0, 4, 0, 0, 2, 2, 0, 4, 4), (0, 4, 0, 0, 0, 3, 1, 0, 0, 0, 3, 1, 0, 4, 4, 0, 4, 0, 0, 3, 1, 0, 4, 4), (0, 4, 0, 0, 0, 4, 0, 0, 0, 0, 4, 0, 0, 4, 4, 0, 4, 0, 0, 4, 0, 0, 4, 4), (0, 4, 0, 0, 0, 1, 3, 0, 0, 1, 0, 3, 1, 3, 4, 0, 4, 0, 0, 1, 3, 1, 3, 4), (0, 4, 0, 0, 0, 2, 2, 0, 0, 1, 1, 2, 1, 3, 4, 0, 4, 0, 0, 2, 2, 1, 3, 4), (0, 4, 0, 0, 0, 3, 1, 0, 0, 1, 2, 1, 1, 3, 4, 0, 4, 0, 0, 3, 1, 1,$

Table 2. The availability, cost, coverage set and SI for the example.

Op.	Avail.	Cost (in $\$10^3$)	P_i	Coverage sets	SI
a_1	0.98	0.8	$\{mp_1, mp_2, mp_3, mp_4\}$	$\{a_1, a_3, a_4, a_5, a_8, a_9, a_{16}, a_{18}, a_{19}\}$	0.375
a_2	0.98	0.8	$\{mp_5, mp_6, mp_7\}$	$\{a_2, a_6, a_7, a_{12}, a_{17}, a_{21}\}$	0.25
a_3	0.97	0.6	$\{mp_1\}$	$\{a_3, a_8, a_{18}\}$	0.042
a_4	0.97	0.6	$\{mp_2\}$	$\{a_4, a_9, a_{19}\}$	0.042
a_5	0.97	0.6	$\{mp_3, mp_4\}$	$\{a_5\}$	0.042
a_6	0.97	0.6	$\{mp_5, mp_6\}$	$\{a_6\}$	0.042
a_7	0.97	0.6	$\{mp_7\}$	$\{a_7, a_{12}, a_{21}\}$	0.042
a_8	0.96	0.7	$\{mp_1\}$	$\{a_3, a_8, a_{18}\}$	0.042
a_9	0.96	0.7	$\{mp_2\}$	$\{a_4, a_9, a_{19}\}$	0.042
a_{10}	0.96	0.7	$\{mp_3, mp_5\}$	$\{a_{10}\}$	0.042
a_{11}	0.96	0.7	$\{mp_4, mp_6\}$	$\{a_{11}\}$	0.042
a_{12}	0.96	0.7	$\{mp_7\}$	$\{a_7, a_{12}, a_{21}\}$	0.042
a_{13}	0.95	0.8	$\{mp_1, mp_2, mp_3, mp_5\}$	$\{a_3, a_4, a_8, a_9, a_{10}, a_{13}, a_{18}, a_{19}, a_{22}\}$	0.375
a_{14}	0.95	0.8	$\{mp_4, mp_6, mp_7\}$	$\{a_7, a_{11}, a_{12}, a_{14}, a_{21}, a_{23}\}$	0.25
a_{15}	0.96	1.1	$\{mp_1, mp_2, mp_3, mp_4, mp_5, mp_6, mp_7\}$	$\{a_1, a_2, a_3, a_4, a_5, a_6, a_7, a_8, a_9, a_{10}, a_{11}, a_{12}, a_{13}, a_{14}, a_{15}, a_{16}, a_{17}, a_{18}, a_{19}, a_{20}, a_{21}, a_{22}, a_{23}, a_{24}\}$	1.0
a_{16}	0.94	1.2	$\{mp_1, mp_2, mp_3, mp_4\}$	$\{a_1, a_3, a_4, a_5, a_8, a_9, a_{16}, a_{18}, a_{19}\}$	0.375
a_{17}	0.94	1.2	$\{mp_5, mp_6, mp_7\}$	$\{a_2, a_6, a_7, a_{12}, a_{17}, a_{21}\}$	0.25
a_{18}	0.94	1.2	$\{mp_1\}$	$\{a_3, a_8, a_{18}\}$	0.042
a_{19}	0.94	1.2	$\{mp_2\}$	$\{a_4, a_9, a_{19}\}$	0.042
a_{20}	0.94	1.2	$\{mp_3, mp_4, mp_5, mp_6\}$	$\{a_5, a_6, a_{10}, a_{11}, a_{20}\}$	0.208
a_{21}	0.94	1.2	$\{mp_7\}$	$\{a_7, a_{12}, a_{21}\}$	0.042
a_{22}	0.97	1.3	$\{mp_1, mp_2, mp_3, mp_5\}$	$\{a_3, a_4, a_8, a_9, a_{10}, a_{18}, a_{19}, a_{22}\}$	0.333
a_{23}	0.97	1.3	$\{mp_4, mp_6, mp_7\}$	$\{a_7, a_{11}, a_{12}, a_{14}, a_{21}, a_{23}\}$	0.25
a_{24}	0.99	1.0	$\{mp_1, mp_2, mp_3, mp_4, mp_5, mp_6, mp_7\}$	$\{a_1, a_2, a_3, a_4, a_5, a_6, a_7, a_8, a_9, a_{10}, a_{11}, a_{12}, a_{13}, a_{14}, a_{15}, a_{16}, a_{17}, a_{18}, a_{19}, a_{20}, a_{21}, a_{22}, a_{23}, a_{24}\}$	1.0

$3, 4), (0 , 4, 0, 0, 0, 4, 0, 0, 0, 1, 3, 0, 1, 3, 4, 0, 4, 0, 0, 4, 0, 1,$
$3, 4), (0, 4, 0, 0, 0, 2, 2, 0, 0, 2, 0, 2, 2, 2, 4, 0, 4, 0, 0, 2, 2, 2,$
$2, 4), (0, 4, 0, 0, 0, 3, 1, 0, 0, 2, 1, 1, 2, 2, 4, 0, 4, 0, 0, 3, 1, 2,$
$2, 4), (0, 4, 0, 0, 0, 4, 0, 0, 0, 2, 2, 0, 2, 2, 4, 0, 4, 0, 0, 4, 0, 2,$
$2, 4), (0, 4, 0, 0, 0, 3, 1, 0, 0, 3, 0, 1, 3, 1, 4, 0, 4, 0, 0, 3, 1, 3,$
$1, 4), (0, 4, 0, 0, 0, 4, 0, 0, 0, 3, 1, 0, 3, 1, 4, 0, 4, 0, 0, 4, 0, 3,$
$1, 4), (0, 4, 0, 0, 0, 4, 0, 0, 0, 4, 0, 0, 4, 0, 4, 0, 4, 0, 0, 4, 0, 4,$
$0, 4)\}.$

iii. Generate $\Omega_{min,1}$ via simple comparison. //i.e., pairwise comparison.

$\Omega_{min,1} = \{(0, 4, 0, 0, 0, 0, 4, 0, 0, 0, 0, 4, 0, 4, 4, 0, 4, 0, 0, 0,$
$4, 0, 4, 4), (0, 4, 0, 0, 0, 1, 3, 0, 0, 0, 1, 3, 0, 4, 4, 0, 4, 0, 0, 1,$
$3, 0, 4, 4), (0, 4, 0, 0, 0, 2, 2, 0, 0, 0, 2, 2, 0, 4, 4, 0, 4, 0, 0, 2,$
$2, 0, 4, 4), (0, 4, 0, 0, 0, 3, 1, 0, 0, 0, 3, 1, 0, 4, 4, 0, 4, 0, 0, 3,$
$1, 0, 4, 4), (0, 4, 0, 0, 0, 4, 0, 0, 0, 0, 4, 0, 0, 4, 4, 0, 4, 0, 0, 4,$
$0, 0, 4, 4), (0, 4, 0, 0, 0, 1, 3, 0, 0, 1, 0, 3, 1, 3, 4, 0, 4, 0, 0, 1,$
$3, 1, 3, 4), (0, 4, 0, 0, 0, 2, 2, 0, 0, 1, 1, 2, 1, 3, 4, 0, 4, 0, 0, 2,$
$2, 1, 3, 4), (0, 4, 0, 0, 0, 3, 1, 0, 0, 1, 2, 1, 1, 3, 4, 0, 4, 0, 0, 3,$
$1, 1, 3, 4), (0, 4, 0, 0, 0, 4, 0, 0, 0, 1, 3, 0, 1, 3, 4, 0, 4, 0, 0, 4,$
$0, 1, 3, 4), (0, 4, 0, 0, 0, 2, 2, 0, 0, 2, 0, 2, 2, 2, 4, 0, 4, 0, 0, 2,$
$2, 2, 2, 4), (0, 4, 0, 0, 0, 3, 1, 0, 0, 2, 1, 1, 2, 2, 4, 0, 4, 0, 0, 3,$
$1, 2, 2, 4), (0, 4, 0, 0, 0, 4, 0, 0, 0, 2, 2, 0, 2, 2, 4, 0, 4, 0, 0, 4,$
$0, 2, 2, 4), (0, 4, 0, 0, 0, 3, 1, 0, 0, 3, 0, 1, 3, 1, 4, 0, 4, 0, 0, 3,$
$1, 3, 1, 4), (0, 4, 0, 0, 0, 4, 0, 0, 0, 3, 1, 0, 3, 1, 4, 0, 4, 0, 0, 4,$
$0, 3, 1, 4), (0, 4, 0, 0, 0, 4, 0, 0, 0, 4, 0, 0, 4, 0, 4, 0, 4, 0, 0, 4,$
$0, 4, 0, 4)\}.$

(b) For $X = (0, 4, 0, 0, 0, 0, 4, 0, 0, 0, 0, 4, 0, 4, 4, 0, 4, 0, 0, 0, 4, 0, 4,$
$4) \in \Omega_{min,1}$ do // The filtering process.

Because $\|\varphi = \{3, 4, 5, 6, 7, 10, 11\} \setminus \{1, 3, 4, 5, 8, 9, 16, 18, 19\}\| = 4 \leq 4$, then for $l = 6$ do if $x_6 = 0$ and $6 \neq 1$ and $6 \notin Q_1$, then $\Omega_{min,1} = \Omega_{min,1} \setminus \{X = (0, 4, 0, 0, 0, 0, 4, 0, 0, 0, 0, 4, 0, 4, 4, 0, 4, 0, 0, 0, 4, 0, 4,$
$4)\}.$

$\vdots$

At the end of the loop: $\Omega_{min,1} = \{(0, 4, 0, 0, 0, 2, 2, 0, 0, 1, 1,$
$2, 1, 3, 4, 0, 4, 0, 0, 2, 2, 1, 3, 4), (0, 4, 0, 0, 0, 3, 1, 0, 0, 1, 2,$
$1, 1, 3, 4, 0, 4, 0, 0, 3, 1, 1, 3, 4), (0, 4, 0, 0, 0, 3, 1, 0, 0, 2, 1,$
$1, 2, 2, 4, 0, 4, 0, 0, 3, 1, 2, 2, 4)\}$.

2. For $i = 1$ do // Construct $M_{i,j}$.

For $X = (0, 4, 0, 0, 0, 2, 2, 0, 0, 1, 1, 2, 1, 3, 4, 0, 4, 0, 0, 2, 2, 1, 3, 4)$ do

Because $x_2 = 4 > 0$ and $x_2 \notin M_{1,2}$, then $M_{1,2} = M_{1,2} \cup \{4\}$.

$\vdots$

At the end of the loop: $M_{1,2} = \{4\}$, $M_{1,6} = \{2,3\}$, $M_{1,7} =$
$\{1,2\}, M_{1,10} = \{1,2\}, M_{1,11} = \{1,2\}, M_{1,12} = \{1,2\}, M_{1,13} =$
$\{1,2\}$, $M_{1,14} = \{2,3\}$, $M_{1,15} = \{4\}$, $M_{1,17} = \{4\}$, $M_{1,20} =$
$\{2,3\}, M_{1,21} = \{1,2\}, M_{1,22} = \{1,2\}, M_{1,23} = \{2,3\}, M_{1,24} =$
$\{4\}$.

3. For $j = 1$ do // Construct $\mathbf{m}_j$.

$M_{min,1} = \max\{1,2,3,4\} = 4$.

$M_{max,1} = \max\{4\} = 4$.

$\mathbf{m}_1 = \{m_j | 4 \leq m_j \leq 4\}$.

$\vdots$

At the end of the loop: $\mathbf{m}_1 = \{4\}$, $\mathbf{m}_2 = \{4\}$, $\mathbf{m}_3 = \{1,2\}$,
$\mathbf{m}_4 = \{1,2\}$, $\mathbf{m}_5 = \{2\}$, $\mathbf{m}_6 = \{2,3\}$, $\mathbf{m}_7 = \{1,2\}$, $\mathbf{m}_8 =$
$\{1,2\}$, $\mathbf{m}_9 = \{1,2\}$, $\mathbf{m}_{10} = \{2\}$, $\mathbf{m}_{11} = \{2,3\}$, $\mathbf{m}_{12} = \{1,2\}$,
$\mathbf{m}_{13} = \{4\}$, $\mathbf{m}_{14} = \{4\}$, $\mathbf{m}_{15} = \{4\}$, $\mathbf{m}_{16} = \{4\}$, $\mathbf{m}_{17} = \{4\}$,
$\mathbf{m}_{18} = \{1,2\}$, $\mathbf{m}_{19} = \{1,2\}$, $\mathbf{m}_{20} = \{2,3\}$, $\mathbf{m}_{21} = \{1,2\}$,
$\mathbf{m}_{22} = \{4\}$, $\mathbf{m}_{23} = \{4\}$, $\mathbf{m}_{24} = \{4\}$.

4. For $M = (4, 1, 1, 2, 2, 1, 1, 1, 2, 2, 1, 4, 4, 4, 4, 4, 1, 1, 1, 2, 1, 4, 4, 4)$ do
// Construct Γ.

set $CNT = 0$.

For $i = 1$ do

For $X = (0, 4, 0, 0, 0, 2, 2, 0, 0, 1, 1, 2, 1, 3, 4, 0, 4, 0, 0, 2, 2, 1, 3, 4)$ do

If $M \geq X$, then $CNT = 0 + 1 = 1$ and break.

$\vdots$

      Finally: $\Gamma = \{(4, 4, 1, 1, 2, 2, 2, 1, 1, 2, 2, 2, 4, 4, 4, 4, 4, 1, 1, 2, 2, 4, 4, 4), \ldots\}$ and has total 617 vectors.

5. Let $sum_C = 1152$. // Here $1152 = 24 * 4 * 12$ denotes a feasible large number.

6. For $M = (4, 4, 1, 1, 2, 2, 2, 1, 1, 2, 2, 2, 4, 4, 4, 4, 4, 1, 1, 2, 2, 4, 4, 4)$ do
   // Search for the optimal M.

   Because $\sum_{j=1}^{24} m_j c_j + 12 \cdot 4(1 - R_4(M)) = 64.2326 < 1152$, then $M_{best} = (4, 4, 1, 1, 2, 2, 2, 1, 1, 2, 2, 2, 4, 4, 4, 4, 4, 1, 1, 2, 2, 4, 4, 4)$ and $sum_C = 64.2326$.

   $\vdots$

         At the end of the loop: $M_{best} = (4, 4, 1, 1, 2, 2, 2, 1, 1, 2, 3, 2, 4, 4, 4, 4, 4, 1, 1, 2, 2, 4, 4, 4)$ and $sum_C = 62.9488$.

9. The optimal plan is $(4, 4, 1, 1, 2, 2, 2, 1, 1, 2, 3, 2, 4, 4, 4, 4, 4, 1, 1, 2, 2, 4, 4, 4)$, the lowest cost is 62.9488 and the performance is $R_4 = 0.928151$.

The optimal capacity plan for this example is $(4, 4, 1, 1, 2, 2, 2, 1, 1, 2, 3, 2, 4, 4, 4, 4, 4, 1, 1, 2, 2, 4, 4, 4)$. This is equivalent to 4 persons for order-entry operation , 1 SAP B1 system, etc. The detailed plan is in Table 3. The minimal cost is 62.9488 (in $\$10^3$). The performance is predicted as $R_4 = 0.928151$, a pretty good level. Such plan can also tolerate absentees as well as machine failures when in operation. This is shown by the following critical analysis comparing with an empirical plan in Table 4.

In this table, there are 16 critical operations in the empirical plan. This means that the major operations can not fail, otherwise the process will be stopped. Because of the high penalty during the operation down time, the empirical plan incurred higher total cost. It is apparent that the proposed plan is superior to the empirical one.

Table 3. Optimal capacity plan corresponding to the staff or machine plan.

Operations Plan	a_1 1 SAP B1	a_2 1 SAP ERP	a_3 1 Conveyor	a_4 1 Conveyor	a_5 1 Conveyor
Operations Plan	a_6 4 Faxes	a_7 1 Conveyor	a_8 1 Truck	a_9 1 Truck	a_{10} 2 Trucks
Operations Plan	a_{11} 1 Boat	a_{12} 2 Trucks	a_{13} 8 Faxes	a_{14} 8 Faxes	a_{15} 4 persons
Operations Plan	a_{16} 4 persons	a_{17} 4 persons	a_{18} 1 MC	a_{19} 1 MC	a_{20} 2 MCs
Operations Plan	a_{21} 2 MCs	a_{22} 8 persons	a_{23} 8 persons	a_{24} 4 persons	

6.   Conclusion

This chapter proposes an algorithm to find the optimal capacity plan in a business process under absentees and machine failures such that the process is robust and the required total cost is minimal while the performance is predictable. Since the globalized economics changes very fast, the uncertainty for each firm is also versatile. Our approach can provide companies a helpful toolkit to manage such uncertainty while keeping the ability to predict the performance of the process. At first, we do the structural analysis as a basis for the plan strategy. The structural analysis is to determine the components which can not fail despite how many resources engaged. Then, such plan are evaluated by the critical analysis which identifies the critical components of the underlined network. A critical component is a component where only its failure causes the system performance dropped to zero. This chapter also demonstrates a numerical example to show the efficiency of the proposed approach.

Table 4. The critical analysis and the comparison with an empirical plan.

Operations	M	Proposed Plan Survivability	Critical?	M	Empirical Plan Survivability	Critical?
a_1	4	0.37334	N	3	0.0	Y
a_2	4	0.374	N	2	0.0	Y
a_3	1	0.9135	N	1	0.5239	N
a_4	1	0.9135	N	1	0.5239	N
a_5	2	0.9422	N	1	0.5292	N
a_6	2	0.8664	N	1	0.0	Y
a_7	2	0.5504	N	1	0.0	Y
a_8	1	0.9135	N	1	0.5239	N
a_9	1	0.9135	N	1	0.5239	N
a_{10}	2	0.9458	N	1	0.5292	N
a_{11}	3	0.8468	N	1	0.0	Y
a_{12}	2	0.5504	N	1	0.0	Y
a_{13}	4	0.3955	N	3	0.0	Y
a_{14}	4	0.3662	N	2	0.0	Y
a_{15}	4	0.0	Y	6	0.0	Y
a_{16}	4	0.3733	N	2	0.0	Y
a_{17}	4	0.374	N	3	0.0	Y
a_{18}	1	0.9135	N	3	0.5239	N
a_{19}	1	0.9135	N	3	0.5239	N
a_{20}	2	0.4776	N	3	0.0	Y
a_{21}	2	0.5504	N	3	0.0	Y
a_{22}	4	0.3955	N	2	0.0	Y
a_{23}	4	0.3662	N	3	0.0	Y
a_{24}	4	0.0	Y	6	0.0	Y
performance $R_4(M)$		0.928151			0.601515	
Cost (in $\$10^3$)		62.9488			73.1273	
Robustness		Yes			No	

Acknowledgement

This work was supported in part by the National Science Council, Taiwan, Republic of China, under Grant No. NSC 98-2221-E-236-011.

References

Anderson Jr., E. G. (2007). The nonstationary staff planning problem with business cycle and learning effects. *Management Science*, **47**(6):817 – 832.

Arbel, A. and Seidmann, A. (1984). Performance evaluation of flexible manufacturing systems. *IEEE Trancsactions on Systems, Men, and Cybernetics*, **SMC-14**(4):606 – 617.

Armstrong, M. (2006). *A Handbook of Human Resource Management Practice*. Kogan Page, London, 10th edition.

Bilgin, S. and Azizoglu, M. (2009). Operation assignment and capacity allocation problem in automated manufacturing systems. *Computers & Industrial Engineering*, **56**:662 – 676.

Chen, S.-G. (2009). Performance evaluation for an ERP system in case of system failures. In *16th ISPE International Conference on Concurrent Engineering*, Taipei, Taiwan.

Chen, S. G. and Lin, Y. K. (2008a). Capacity assignment for a stochastic-flow network based on structural importance. In *Asian International Workshop on Advanced Reliability Modeling*, Taichung, Taiwan.

Chen, S.-G. and Lin, Y.-K. (2008b). An evaluation method for enterprise resource planning systems. *Journal of the Operations Research Society of Japan*, **51**(4):299–309.

Chen, S.-G. and Lin, Y.-K. (2009). On performance evaluation of ERP systems with fuzzy mathematics. *Expert Systems with Applications*, **36**(3):6362 – 6367.

Crama, Y. (1997). Combinatorial optimization models for production scheduling in automated manufacturing systems. *European Journal of Operational Research*, **99**:136 – 153.

Eveborn, P. and Ronnqvist, M. (2004). Scheduler – a system for staff planning. *Annals of Operations Research*, **128**:21 – 45.

Ford, L. R. and Fulkerson, D. R. (1962). *Flows in networks*. NJ: Princeton University Press.

Hudson, J. C. and Kapur, K. C. (1983). Reliability analysis for multistate systems with multistate components. *IIE Transactions*, **15**(2):127 – 135.

Jane, C. C. and Laih, Y. W. (2008). A practical algorithm for computing multistate two-terminal reliability. *IEEE Transactions on Reliability*, 57(2):295 – 302.

Lawler, J. P., Benedict, V., Howell-Barber, H., and Joseph, A. (2009). Critical success factors in the planning of a service-oriented architecture (SOA) strategy for educators and managers. *Information Systems Education Journal*, **7**:1 – 30.

Lin, Y.-K. (2001). A simple algorithm for reliability evaluation of a stochastic-flow network with node failure. *Computers and Operations Research*, **28**(13):1277 – 1285.

Nagalingam, S. V. and Lin, G. C. I. (1998). A methodology to select optimal system components for computer integrated manufacturing by evaluating synergy. *Computer Integrated Manufacturing Systems*, 11(3):217 – 238.

Perrone, G., Amico, M., Lo Nigro, G., and La Diega, S. N. (2002). Long term capacity decisions in uncertain markets for advanced manufacturing systems incorporating scope economics. *European Journal of Operational Research*, **143**:125 – 137.

Yeh, W. C. (2005). A novel method for the network reliability in terms of capacitated-minimum-paths without knowing minimum-paths in advance. *Journal of the Operational Research Society*, **56**(10):1235 – 1240.

INDEX